EASYMADE WINE
AND
COUNTRY DRINKS

Other *Paperfronts* of interest:

EASYMADE WINE

AND

COUNTRY DRINKS

By

MRS. GENNERY-TAYLOR

Revised by Bill Cook of U-Brew-it

PAPERFRONTS

ELLIOT RIGHT WAY BOOKS
KINGSWOOD, SURREY, U.K.

Made and Printed in Great Britain
by Cox & Wyman Ltd, London,
Reading and Fakenham

PREFACE

THIS book is intended for the ordinary housewife or perhaps her husband.

I hope it will be helpful to those who wish to make a few bottles for home consumption or for giving to friends.

I have tried to show that good wine can be made in small quantities and with simple equipment. I therefore hope my book will encourage some of you to start this fascinating hobby.

I should also like to thank those friends who have so kindly let me use their own special recipes.

I affectionately dedicate this book to my parents and to Charles for suggesting it, I say, 'thank you'.

CONTENTS

PART I: GENERAL INSTRUCTIONS

	PAGE
HINTS ON WINEMAKING	9
ECONOMY	10
UTENSILS AND CONTAINERS	10
FORMING A MOULD	12
STERILIZATION	12
THE WINEFLY	13
FERMENTATION	13
CLEARING THE WINE	14
STRAINING THE WINE	14
USING THE FERMENTATION JAR	14
RACKING	16
STORING WINE	16
YEASTS	17
BASIC AMOUNTS AND METHODS	17

PART II: WINES

WINES AS REMEDIES	19
CHRISTMAS DRINKS	20
A CALENDAR FOR WINEMAKING	22

CONTENTS

PART III: WINE RECIPES

PAGE

63 WINE RECIPES 25

PART IV: OTHER DRINKS

BLACKBERRY CORDIAL 91

GINGER BEER 92

MEAD 93

CIDER 94

BEER 96

FRUIT SYRUPS. 7 RECIPES 99

PART V: CHILDREN'S DRINKS, TEAS AND COFFEES

CHILDREN'S DRINKS. 10 RECIPES . . . 107

HERB TEAS. 15 RECIPES 119

DANDELION COFFEE 125

INDEX 126

PART I
GENERAL INSTRUCTIONS
—
HINTS ON WINEMAKING

SOON after I married I decided to make some wine. I had never made any and had no idea how to begin. I remembered that my grandmother used to make excellent wine, but I was a child then – too young to learn.

I was lucky, however, in having a good friend who could make wine. To her it was an inherited accomplishment, handed down from one generation to another, as necessary to housekeeping and cooking.

She gave me a recipe for rhubarb wine and as it was springtime there was plenty of rhubarb about. I followed her directions carefully and found everything absurdly simple. But still I didn't believe that this fruit juice could become wine.

I filled the wine bottles and placed them in a cool dark cupboard. Never was a wine watched so carefully. I inspected and tasted it nearly every day. Hapless visitors were forced to try it, but my husband revolted – he would rather wait till it was ready to drink.

Somehow I managed to save two bottles for six months and found, secretly to my surprise, that it had turned into a very pleasant wine. This greatly encouraged me, and I began to make different kinds and have done so ever since.

Of course I had some failures, sometimes I was careless and the winefly got in and turned the wine sour.

Other times I left too much airspace in the fermentation

jars and the wine turned sharp. But gradually I learned to be careful and watch for these things.

Although we are not constantly drinking wine, I rarely seem to keep a bottle for much more than a year to mature properly. I firmly hide several bottles, but there is always that special occasion which seems to demand a bottle of wine. So my stock dwindles.

I love trying new recipes or inventing my own.

I FIND THAT THE MAIN VIRTUE NEEDED FOR WINEMAKING IS PATIENCE.

ECONOMY

One thing that consoles me when I see my wine disappearing so quickly is that it is much cheaper than shop wine.

I believe that home-made wine can cost less than a tenth of the price of the cheapest shop wine. In many cases, where wild fruits or flowers are gathered, sugar is the only ingredient to be bought. So this wine costs no more than a few pence a bottle.

One can also be extravagant in using it for cooking. Home-made wines can often take the place of white wine or sherry. There is no need to use the wine sparingly when one knows there are some more bottles in the cellar.

UTENSILS AND CONTAINERS

Please do not be put off making wine by the thought of the expensive equipment to be bought. Most of us have a large saucepan or preserving pan which will do to boil those ingredients which need boiling.

METAL CONTAINERS MAY BE USED AT THIS STAGE, *BUT MUST NEVER BE USED TO HOLD*

FERMENTING WINE (EXCEPT STAINLESS STEEL).

Next you need a large bowl, a big earthenware mixing bowl will do. A plastic bucket makes an excellent container for your mix, because it is light, easily cleaned and easy to cover. To have two buckets is a great advantage.

Bottles are the next item. Keep all your old lemonade or wine bottles, those with corks are the best. Most types hold just over a pint of wine.

The only other things you will need are a wooden or plastic spoon for stirring and a piece of butter muslin or fine net for straining. So the following articles are all you really require:

   1 large saucepan or preserving pan.
   2 large earthenware bowls or plastic buckets.
   A wooden or plastic spoon.
   A piece of butter muslin or straining bag.
   A plastic funnel.

If you wish to make sufficient wine to be able to enjoy it freely and to build up a mature stock for special occasions, it is advisable to make not less than a gallon at a time: $1\frac{1}{2}$ or 2 gals. can be made with very little extra effort and therefore a 2 gal. or $2\frac{1}{4}$ gal. bucket is worth having.

Earthenware crocks, formerly used, are becoming scarce; they are comparatively expensive, heavy and harder to handle. Wooden casks are favoured by advanced amateur winemakers fortunate enough to possess them, but they require careful use and are certainly not essential, as good wine can be made with the simple equipment specified in this book.

Other very useful containers are gallon jars, which save space, as they will hold six bottles of wine.

11

Glass jars or plastic containers, also corks to fit them, and small plastic fermentation locks, can be obtained from your local Specialists Shop. They are inexpensive and preferable to earthenware jars because it is possible to see exactly how fermentation is progressing. A fermentation lock is a simple device which permits gas to escape through water but prevents air from entering.

FORMING A MOULD

In the first stage of some wines, the fruit has to be left in the bowl until a mould has formed on the top. This should be removed in one piece if possible. Try to avoid little pieces breaking off into the wine.

Sloe wine can be left for months until a really thick mould has formed. Country people say of sloe wine, 'The better the mould, the better the wine.'

Wine often looks rather unpleasant at this stage, especially the flower wines. It doesn't seem possible that this horrible concoction can turn into a clear, sparkling wine. I can assure you it can, so don't be discouraged.

STERILIZATION

It is important that all utensils and bottles used in making and storing wine should be thoroughly sterilized. Washing with boiling water is not good enough. Obtain from your specialist shop or chemist, 4 oz of sodium meta-bisulphite. Dissolve this in one quart of water and pour into a quart bottle and keep corked. This solution can be repeatedly used to sterilize all equipment provided the bottle is kept corked after use. Wash your equipment first, then rinse with the sodium meta-bisulphite solution for sterilization.

THE WINEFLY

Wines fermenting in bowls or other containers must always be covered closely with a clean cloth to prevent the winefly from entering. This tiny fly appears almost from nowhere, it seems, at the mere whiff of fermenting wine. If it does get into the wine in large numbers it will soon turn it sour, so be most careful to keep the bowl completely covered.

FERMENTATION

Throughout this book, sugar is an ingredient in every recipe. In countries where sugar may be scarce, glucose (wheat sugar) has the same fermentation qualities as granulated sugar and can be used instead. It should be used weight for weight (1 lb. of glucose for 1 lb. of sugar).

Fermentation begins in the large container, after sugar and yeast have been added; it requires some warmth and an air space below the covering material; therefore at this stage keep the container in a place where the temperature is 70° – 75° Fahrenheit; e.g., alongside an all night burning stove or radiator. If the container is nearly full some liquid will froth over.

One can tell if wine is fermenting by listening, as a faint hissing noise will be heard. In a clear glass jar, masses of tiny bubbles will be seen rising if held up to the light.

Another test is to put a little sugar in the bottle. If the wine has finished working or fermenting, then nothing will happen. If it is still fermenting the sugar will make it fizz, often right over the top of the bottle. This shows that the yeast in the wine still needs feeding, so add a little sugar.

When you are sure the wine has finished fermenting, it can be finally bottled; push the corks in tightly and put the bottles away to mature for as long as possible. It will keep for years.

CLEARING THE WINE

Wines should clear themselves in time, but to make sure, a little isinglass may be added while the wine is still fermenting.

Dissolve $\frac{1}{4}$ oz. of isinglass in a cup of water and pour gently into a gallon of wine.

This is not essential, and I have never used it, because even a stubborn wine clears in its own time. However, if you wish to hasten the process, then isinglass is the answer.

STRAINING THE WINE

I find butter muslin the best material for straining wines. Straining is most easily done by laying the muslin across a plastic flour sifter (borrowed from kitchen); lodging the sifter across a plastic bucket and pouring the wine through.

On no account use a metal strainer as this could react to the acid in the wine and would probably turn it black.

USING THE FERMENTATION JAR

The strained wine is then transferred into a fermentation jar by using a plastic funnel. These jars can be made of

14

glass or non-toxic plastic. If the wine is fermenting vigorously, do not fill to the top of the jar as it might froth over. Fit an air-lock or stuff the opening with cotton wool to prevent the air from getting in. When the fermentation has subsided somewhat, fill the jar to within one inch of the base of the bung and allow the must (fermenting wine) to continue until the fermentation has stopped.

The odd half bottle of liquid which is usually left over can be used for filling the jar. You will find sometimes, that after the wine has been fermenting, the level in the jar has sunk a little. Fill the jar up from the spare bottle. This small amount will not keep long if left in a large bottle, as the airspace will turn it sour. I find it better to keep this spare wine in a small bottle, such as a medicine bottle. When a bottle of wine is opened for use, it should not be kept more than a few weeks as it will go sour.

In the recipes that follow, the periods specified for transfer to jars after sugar and yeast have been added, vary from 3 to 14 days; these are minimum periods and more time can be allowed safely and profitably, provided that the original container is covered effectively.

It is advisable to test the state of the fermentation with a hydrometer. This simple instrument measures the quantity of sugar in the must and can be obtained, at a very reasonable cost, at any specialist shop. When the fermentation stops, there may be too much sugar left, giving a sweet wine that is undrinkable. This is what would happen if too much sugar had been put in in the first place. By using the hydrometer one can determine whether the wine has fermented to dryness (no sugar left), and then, if the wine is too dry for personal taste, sweeten with sugar before bottling.

RACKING

When fermentation is apparently finished and the wine has cleared, it is time to put the wine into its final bottles and cork firmly. It is a simple operation to syphon off the clear wine with a thin plastic tube without disturbing the sediment or lees, which will be visible at the bottom of the bottles or glass jars. This process is known as racking.

Some wines take much longer than others to clear, but it is pointless to rack them beforehand, and it is here that patience is essential.

Also, it is important to make sure that the wine is stable, i.e., not fermenting before you bottle.

STORING WINE

Ideally, wine should be stored in a cool dark place, preferably on a stone floor, at a temperature of 55° Fahrenheit. But it survives quite well under less perfect conditions. So don't worry if you live in a flat with no nice cool cellar or pantry. Find a cupboard that is not too near a fireplace, and use that.

IT IS BEST TO INSPECT THE BOTTLES FAIRLY OFTEN AS THE CORKS DO SOMETIMES POP OUT, THEN THE LITTLE WINEFLY POPS IN AND TURNS THE WINE SOUR.

It has been suggested that the wine bottles should be turned on their sides as professional wine-makers do. This might, however, be difficult in the home where storage space is often limited. I think if the bottles are filled and the corks pushed in tightly this should prevent the corks from drying out and shrinking and so letting in the air. As a precaution, the tops of the corks may be waxed.

YEASTS

The yeasts I have included in the recipes are general purpose wine yeasts. Dried yeasts which are easily obtainable nowadays are equally effective. (It is only for beer that Brewers' yeast is advised.) For those who can afford it, however, special selected wine yeasts in dry or liquid form can be obtained. It is claimed that the use of these brings out the maximum bouquet and alcoholic qualities of the wine as well as making the clarifying easier. They are obtainable from your local specialist shop.

These shops specialise in the supply of home-made wine equipment and a visit to their premises or a request for their catalogue is an education.

BASIC AMOUNTS AND METHODS

You may find you wish to make wine from some fruit, flower or vegetable not mentioned in this book. The general rule then is:

For flower and fruit wines:

Pour the boiling water over the fruit or flowers and leave to stand for about a week, then strain and add the sugar and yeast.

For root wines:

The ingredients are usually boiled. Then strained over the sugar, and the yeast added when the wine is lukewarm. The proportions are roughly:

3 or 4 lbs. of fruit

2½ or 3 lbs. of sugar

1 gallon of water.

These vary with different wines and very often other ingredients are added to provide flavour.

If it is a wine that simmers, use about fifty percent more water to allow for evaporation.

Halving the ingredients to make less wine will not affect its strength.

You will need to experiment a little, but if you follow these main rules you can't go far wrong.

Wine connoisseurs will like to take note that the recipes contained in this book *are* country wines and for that reason tend towards being sweet wines. If you desire your wine to have a drier taste, you can reduce the amount of sugar in any of the wine recipes to accord with your personal taste. However, you should never reduce the amount below 2 lb. of sugar.

In most of the recipes you will find G.P. wine yeast, yeast nutrient, and/or pectic enzyme are called for. It is not possible to set the amount of these substances on the recipes because, depending where you have bought them, they may have different working strengths per amount. However, the right quantity to use is always stated on the packet or tub, etc., and the manufacturers' instructions can be reliably followed.

PART II
WINES

—

WINES AS REMEDIES

YEARS ago, many people depended almost entirely on home-made remedies for their ailments. Quite a number of country people today still believe in them implicitly. Wines are quite important in this role and are a very pleasant way of taking medicine. I am sure if doctors' medicines were so delicious, the Health Service would collapse entirely!

Here are some wines which are, so I am told, safe and certain cures. Anyway a glass of wine at any time is a great morale lifter and may help one to forget one's aches and pains. I must, however, warn those who suffer from rheumatism, that they should never touch rhubarb wine.

Cowslip wine will cure jaundice.

Dandelion is good for indigestion and kidney trouble.

Sloe wine is effective for diarrhoea.

Elderberry wine taken hot on a cold morning will ward off colds.

Raspberry wine is invaluable for sore throats.

Blackcurrant wine when mulled is excellent for colds and bronchitis.

Barley wine is good for kidney trouble.

And Rhubarb wine is bad for rheumatism.

CHRISTMAS DRINKS

At Christmas the drinks seem to disappear like magic What with parties, odd callers and extra drinks for the family one needs to spend a fortune to keep up with the demand. Unless, of course, one had home-made wine to fall back on.

But I admit, to offer a visitor a glass of home-made wine at the festive season may seem rather tame, so I dress up my drinks a little. I have found that with a little experimenting I can make quite a good wine cocktail with my own wine. I will write out one or two to give you an example, but it only needs a little mixing and tasting to improvise a drink with what you have at hand.

LUCKY DIP

The first one I call "Lucky Dip".

$\frac{1}{2}$ bottle of rhubarb wine.
$\frac{1}{2}$ bottle of marrow wine.
1 wineglass of ginger wine.
1 wineglass of whisky.
1 wineglass of rum.
1 tumbler of carrot wine.
1 tumbler of ginger beer.

Just mix them all together; it sounds a strange mixture, but tastes good.

"GUESS WHAT"

$\frac{1}{2}$ bottle blackberry wine.
$\frac{1}{2}$ bottle rhubarb wine.
1 wineglass ginger wine.
1 wineglass port wine.

½ wineglass whisky.
Mix together and you have the answer!

ORANGE COCKTAIL

1 bottle orange wine.
1 wineglass whisky.
Dash of rum.

OTHER HINTS

If you prefer brandy or gin as the spirit content just experiment a little using these; of course you can be more extravagant with the spirits if you wish, but as a general party drink I find those I have mentioned quite adequate.

If you have a favourite punch recipe, which needs a bottle of sherry or other wine, substitute a bottle of home-made wine or use half and half.

I had a bottle of beetroot wine which was not really old enough to drink, but I wanted a red wine, so I poured a glass of port into the decanter and poured the beet wine on to it. The flavour was improved and several people praised the wine.

My marrow wine, although quite strong already, I thought could do with a fillip for the party season. So to one bottle I added a glass of whisky and to another a glass of rum and corked them down till required. One visitor after having two glasses of the rum marrow wine said he felt quite tipsy on going out into the air and was jolly all the way home.

So, if like me you have to economise at times remember these tips. It requires little spirits or port and it is so much nicer to be able to serve out drinks with a liberal hand, instead of with one eye on the bottle all the time.

A CALENDAR FOR WINEMAKING

It is often hard, especially if one happens to live in a town, to remember when the time is for making various wines. People who live in the country are more fortunate as they can see when the different flowers and fruits are ready.

This calendar will act as a reminder. Town folk on a fine day can pack their lunch and sally forth to the country in search of the fruits and flowers of the fields and hedgerows. The country folk can just step outside their doors any day and help themselves, to the wild flowers and fruits at least: not, I hope, to the farmer's wheat or sugar beet!

There are wines to make in every month, plenty to keep the most industrious person busy, but I don't think many people could find the storage space for so many different varieties. However, if you can only try a few, there should be enough to ensure a Merry Christmas.

The dried fruit wines can, of course, be made all the year round. I have only included them in the winter months when there are not so many varieties of fruit and vegetables to be found.

The weather influences the season of the flowers and fruits. In a cold year they may be late, and in a warm year a bit earlier, but it doesn't vary more than a week or so. Some things such as grapes and pears can be bought at any time in the shops, but the out-of-season varieties are too expensive for wine.

WINE CALENDAR

January
Potato, Wheat, Barley, Raisin, Ginger, Fig, Dried Apricot, Dried Peach, Orange.

22

February

Potato, Wheat, Barley, Raisin, Lemon, Fig, Parsnip, Dried Apricot, Dried Peach, Ginger.

March

Coltsfoot, Lemon, Tea, Parsnip, Turnip, Potato, Carrot, Barley, Dried Fruits.

April

Dandelion, Parsnip, Turnip, Carrot, Tea, Ginger, Dried Fruits.

May

Dandelion, Rhubarb, Marigold, Cowslip, Elderflower, Gooseberry.

June

Strawberry, Marigold, Dandelion, Elderflower, Rhubarb, Gooseberry, Plum.

July

Blackcurrant, Redcurrant, Raspberry, Cherry (Clove Carnation), Plum, Bullace.

August

Peach, Apricot, Loganberry, Pear, Plum, Grape, Bullace, Carnation, Marigold, Mulberry, Damson.

September

Grape, Pear, Plum, Damson, Blackberry, Carrot, Beetroot, Marrow, Quince, Mulberry, Elderberry.

October

Apple, Blackberry, Hip, Haw, Grape, Sloe, Sugar Beet, Marrow, Carrot, Elderberry, Turnip, Quince, Beetroot.

November

Apple, Sugar Beet, Marrow, Mangel, Potato, Orange, Wheat, Barley, Carrot, Lemon, Tea.

December

Orange, Lemon, Rice, Apple, Tea, Wheat, Barley, Raisin, Dried Apricot, Dried Peach, Fig, Ginger.

PART III
WINE RECIPES

—

APPLE WINE

3½ lb. cooking apples.
2½ lb. granulated sugar.
1 gallon cold water.
2 lemons.
1 orange.
G.P. wine yeast.
Yeast nutrient.
Pectic enzyme.

Wash the apples and cut out any bad places. Do not peel or core but cut the apples into pieces and put them through the mincer. Now put the minced apples in a plastic bucket and pour 1 gallon of cold water over them.

Cover the bucket and leave for a week, but stir well every day using a plastic spoon. After the week strain the liquid off through muslin into another plastic bucket.

Add the 2½ lb. of granulated sugar and the juice and grated rind of the two lemons and one orange. Stir well until the sugar has dissolved, add the yeast, yeast nutrient and pectic enzyme, then cover the bucket and leave for twenty-four hours. It will then be ready to strain and put into a fermentation jar.

This is a delicious fruit drink when it is first made – my

25

children simply love it – and it is quite safe for them as it doesn't start to turn into a wine for a week or so. If you can leave it for four months you will find it has turned into a very clear, pleasant tasting wine.

FRESH APRICOT WINE

4 lb. fresh apricots
  (weigh after stoning).
3 lb. granulated sugar.
1 gallon boiling water.
G.P. wine yeast.
Yeast nutrient.
Pectic enzyme.

Stone the apricots, cut them into small pieces, and place these in a plastic bucket.

Pour a gallon of boiling water over them and stir well. When cool add yeast, yeast nutrient, and pectic enzyme. Stir every day for five days.

Strain through muslin into another plastic bucket. Add the 3 lb. of sugar and stir daily for three days. Don't forget to keep the bucket covered except when stirring.

The wine is now ready to strain into a fermentation jar. Fit an air-lock and place in the warm until fermentation is finished. Rack into another jar to clear before bottling.

Make sure the jar is kept filled, for you may lose some of the wine by fermentation causing it to fizz over the top. Keep a spare bottle to fill these.

Taste the wine now and again, and if you think it needs some more sugar it won't hurt to add a little.

Store in a cool, dark place and leave for at least six months before drinking.

DRIED APRICOT WINE

2 lb. dried apricots.
3 lb. granulated sugar.
1 gallon boiling water.
G.P. wine yeast.
Yeast nutrient.
Pectic enzyme.
2 Campden tablets.

Wash the 2 lb. of dried apricots and place in a large bowl. Cover with boiling water, crush in two Campden tablets and allow to cool. Add in the pectic enzyme and soak for 36 hours, stirring twice daily. Add the yeast, yeast nutrient and 3 lb. sugar. Ferment on the fruit for four days, stirring daily. Strain into a fermentation jar and leave until fermentation has finished. Rack into another jar and allow to clear. Bottle and store in a cool place. The wine will be ready to drink in nine months.

The apricots left after straining off the liquid will make jam if some sugar is added – about 4 or 5 lb. Make it in the usual way for dried apricot jam, adding a little water, of course.

BARLEY WINE

1½ lb. barley.
1 lemon.
1 orange.
3 lb. granulated sugar.
½ teaspoon ground
  ginger.
1½ gallons cold water.
G.P. wine yeast.
Yeast nutrient.

Put the barley into a large saucepan or preserving pan, and pour on 1½ gallons of cold water. Place over heat and bring to the boil. Simmer for about half an hour, then strain through muslin into a plastic bucket.

Add the sliced lemon and orange, 3 lb. granulated sugar and ½ teaspoon ground ginger. Stir well until the sugar has dissolved.

When the liquid is still lukewarm, stir in the G.P. wine yeast and yeast nutrient. Cover the bucket and leave for fourteen days, then strain and put into a fermentation jar.

This wine will need feeding occasionally with sugar; put a little in each jar every three weeks or so.

When the fermentation has ceased, rack into another jar and allow to clear before bottling. You can drink the wine after six months, but it improves with age. Keep it a year or so and it will become very strong; a wine really worth drinking.

BEETROOT WINE

3 lb. beetroot.
3 lb. granulated sugar.
6 cloves.
G.P. wine yeast.
Yeast nutrient.
1½ gallons cold water.

Wash the beetroot well, but do not peel. Cut it into thin slices and put into a saucepan or preserving pan with the 1½ gallons of water. Bring it to the boil and simmer until the beetroot is tender but not mashy.

Strain off the liquid, and throw away the beetroot, or remove the skin and cover with pepper, salt and vinegar and eat it. Put the liquid back into the saucepan, add the 3 lb. sugar and six cloves and heat just enough to melt the sugar: stir well all the time.

Let the liquid cool until it is lukewarm, then pour it into a plastic bucket. Add the yeast and yeast nutrient. Cover the bucket carefully and leave for three days, stirring daily. Strain the wine into a fermentation jar and ferment until dry. When fermentation has finished, rack into another jar to clear before bottling.

It should be ready to drink in six months, but the longer you keep it the better it will be.

BLACKBERRY WINE (BRAMBLE)

3 lb. blackberries.
3 lb. granulated sugar.
1 gallon boiling water.
G.P. wine yeast.
Yeast nutrient.
Pectic enzyme.

Gather the fruit when ripe on a dry sunny day. Wash the berries to remove any maggots which so often get into blackberries.

Place the blackberries in a large plastic bucket and pour over a gallon of boiling water. Stir well, then cover the bucket and leave for ten days.

Strain the liquid off carefully through muslin making sure that no pips or pulp get through. Add the 3 lb. granulated sugar, the yeast, yeast nutrient and pectic enzyme and stir well. Cover the bucket and leave for another three days, but stir daily.

Transfer into a fermentation jar and allow fermentation to continue until dry. Rack and clear the wine before bottling.

This wine should be ready to drink in six months. It is a lovely dark red wine and rather sweet. If you can add a glass of port or ruby wine to the bottle just before drinking, you will find it hard to tell the difference between this and the shop wine.

BLACKCURRANT WINE

> 4 lb. blackcurrants.
> 3 lb. granulated sugar.
> 1 gallon cold water.
> G.P. wine yeast.
> Yeast nutrient.
> Pectic enzyme.

Strip the blackcurrants from the stalks and wash them carefully so as not to lose too much of the juice.

Put them in a plastic bucket and crush them well using a wooden spoon. Pour on a gallon of cold water and stir thoroughly.

Cover the bucket and leave for ten days, but no longer. Then strain and add the 3 lb. of granulated sugar, the yeast, yeast nutrient and pectic enzyme. Stir daily for three days, then strain into a fermentation jar.

It should be ready to drink in six months.

ANOTHER METHOD

Some people prefer to make this wine with boiling water. Use the same ingredients and quantities.

Wash the fruit and put it into a plastic bucket but do not crush it. Pour on a gallon of boiling water.

Cover the bucket and stand for ten days, then strain and add 3 lb. of granulated sugar and the yeast etc. Stir until it has dissolved, then cover the bucket and leave for another three days, stirring daily. Then strain into a fermentation jar until dry. The wine can then be racked and bottled in the usual way.

Ready in six months.

BULLACE PLUM WINE

4 lb. bullaces.
3 lb. granulated sugar.
1 gallon boiling water.
G.P. wine yeast.
Yeast nutrient.
Pectic enzyme.

Bullaces are best when picked after a frost. Wash the fruit and place it in a plastic bucket.

Pour over the fruit a gallon of boiling water and stir well with a wooden spoon.

Cover the bucket and leave for about three weeks, or until a thick mould has formed.

Remove the mould carefully, in one piece if possible, and strain the liquid off into another bucket. Add 3 lb. of granulated sugar, yeast, yeast nutrient and pectic enzyme and stir well until the sugar has melted. Cover the bucket again and leave for three days.

The wine is then ready to strain into a fermentation jar and ferment until dry. Rack and bottle in the usual way. Store in a cool, dark place.

Try to leave this wine at least a year before drinking, as it needs longer to mature than some wines.

Taste it after a few months, and add a little sugar if you think it needs it. This is a very good wine if left to mature for the full time.

CARROT WINE

4 lb. carrots.
3 lb. granulated sugar.
½ oz. hops.
G.P. wine yeast.
Yeast nutrient.
1 gallon cold water.

Scrub the carrots well and cut them into pieces. Put them in a large preserving pan or saucepan with a gallon of cold water. Boil until the carrots are tender, then strain off the liquid into a plastic bucket. Remove the carrots, then pour the liquid back into the pan and add 3 lb. of granulated sugar and ½ oz. hops. Stir well and just bring to the boil.

Strain into a bucket through muslin to remove the hops, and leave until lukewarm. Add the yeast and nutrient and allow to ferment for a week, stirring twice daily. Keep the bucket covered.

Strain into a fermentation jar, fit airlock, place jar in the warm and ferment until dry. When fermentation has finished, rack into another jar and allow to clear before bottling.

This may need feeding with sugar at intervals of two or three weeks. It will be drinkable in six months, but keep it longer if you can.

CHERRY WINE

5 lb. ripe black cherries.
3 lb. granulated sugar.
1 gallon cold water.
G.P. wine yeast.
Yeast nutrient.
Pectic enzyme.

Remove the stalks from the cherries and wash the fruit. Place the cherries in a large saucepan or preserving pan and crush them with a wooden spoon.

Pour on a gallon of cold water and bring them to the boil. Simmer gently until the cherries are tender, then remove from the heat and strain the liquid off through muslin into a plastic bucket. When you have strained off all the liquid, tip the cherries themselves into the muslin, and squeeze gently to extract any remaining juice.

Add the 3 lb. of granulated sugar and the yeast, yeast nutrient, and pectic enzyme, and stir well. Then cover the bucket and leave for three days, stirring daily. Strain into a fermentation jar, fit an airlock, place the jar in the warm and ferment until dry. When fermentation has finished, rack into another jar and allow to clear before bottling.

You can drink it in six months' time, but keep it longer if you can.

CLOVE CARNATION WINE

2 quarts clove carnations.
3 lb. granulated sugar.
1 gallon boiling water.
G.P. wine yeast.
Yeast nutrient.

Pick the carnations, the clove scented kind, on a sunny day. Use only the heads of the flowers, and wash them well to remove any insects. Measure them in a quart jug and you need two jugs full.

Put the carnation heads into a plastic bucket and pour over them a gallon of boiling water. Stir well.

Cover the bucket and leave for ten days, but stir daily. Strain off the liquid into another bucket and add the 3 lb. of sugar and yeast and yeast nutrient and stir well.

Cover the bucket again and leave for another five days. Strain into a fermentation jar, fit airlock, place in the warm and ferment until dry. When fermentation has finished, rack into another jar to clear before bottling. If the wine is too dry sweeten with sugar.

Keep this wine at least nine months before drinking.

COLTSFOOT WINE

2 quarts of coltsfoot
   flowers.
1 gallon boiling
   water.
½ lb. raisins.
1 lemon.
3 lb. granulated sugar.
G.P. wine yeast.
Yeast nutrient.

Pick the flowers on a sunny day and measure the coltsfoot while fresh. Shake them well to remove any insects.

Put them in a plastic bucket and pour on a gallon of boiling water.

Stir well, then cover the bucket and leave for four days.

Now strain the liquid off into a large saucepan or preserving pan. Add the lemon cut into thin slices and the raisins. Just bring it to the boil.

Pour it all into a plastic bucket and leave until lukewarm. Then stir in the yeast, yeast nutrient and 3 lb. of sugar.

Cover the bucket but stir daily for three days. Then strain into a fermentation jar, fit airlock, place in the warm and ferment until dry. When fermentation has finished, rack into another jar to clear before bottling. Sweeten if necessary.

Ready to drink in six months, but it will improve if you can keep it longer.

COWSLIP WINE

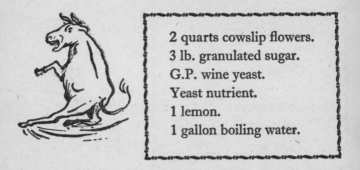

2 quarts cowslip flowers.
3 lb. granulated sugar.
G.P. wine yeast.
Yeast nutrient.
1 lemon.
1 gallon boiling water.

Pick the flowers on a dry day; only the heads are used. Pick the heads of the flowers off, and measure them into a quart jug, but don't press them down. When you have measured two jugs full, wash the flowers well and place in a plastic bucket.

Pour a gallon of boiling water on them, stir well, then cover the bucket and leave for ten days only.

Now strain the liquid off into another bucket and stir in the 3 lb. of granulated sugar, and add the lemon, sliced thinly.

Stir in the G.P. wine yeast and yeast nutrient. Cover the bucket and leave for three days.

Strain into a fermentation jar and ferment until dry. You may find that it needs a little sugar added after a few weeks; drop a little into each bottle.

This can be drunk at once, but will improve with keeping.

Nature conservationists will want to go easy on quantities of Cowslip wine as the pretty yellow flowers have been decreasing rapidly in recent years.

DAMSON WINE. FIRST METHOD

3 lb. ripe damsons.
3 lb. granulated sugar.
1 gallon boiling water.
G.P. wine yeast.
Yeast nutrient.
Pectic enzyme.

Choose ripe damsons, wash them and place in a plastic bucket. Pour over a gallon of boiling water and stir with a plastic spoon. Now cover the bucket and leave until a thick mould has formed on top. This may take weeks, but it doesn't matter as long as you keep the bucket covered. The flavour of the wine will be better if there is a good thick mould.

When you are satisfied that the mould is thick enough, remove it carefully, in one piece if possible. Strain the liquid off into another bucket and add 3 lb. of granulated sugar, yeast, yeast nutrient and pectic enzyme, stir well with a plastic spoon until the sugar has dissolved.

Cover the bucket and leave for three days. Stir daily. Strain into a fermentation jar, place in the warm and ferment until dry. Rack into another jar to clear before bottling.

You can drink it in six months, but it will improve in flavour if you can keep it longer.

DAMSON WINE. SECOND METHOD

> 3 lb. ripe damsons.
> 3 lb. granulated sugar.
> 1 gallon cold water.
> G.P. wine yeast.
> Yeast nutrient.
> Pectic enzyme.

Pick or buy the damsons as ripe as possible and wash them well. Put the 3 lb. damsons in a large saucepan or preserving pan, and pour on a gallon of cold water.

Bring to the boil and simmer until the damsons are tender but not mashy. Strain off the liquid through muslin into a plastic bucket. The damsons can now be used as stewed fruit or for making jam.

Add 3 lb. of granulated sugar to the liquid in the bucket and stir well with a plastic spoon until the sugar has dissolved.

Stir in the yeast, yeast nutrient and pectic enzyme when the liquid is cool to the touch. Transfer into a fermentation jar, fit an airlock and ferment until dry. When the fermentation has stopped, rack into another jar to clear before bottling. Sweeten with sugar if necessary.

You will be able to drink it in six months or perhaps before that. But, the longer you keep it the better it will be.

DANDELION WINE

2 quarts dandelion
    flowers.
3 lb. granulated sugar.
G.P. wine yeast.
Yeast nutrient.
1 lemon.
1 orange.
1 gallon boiling water.

Pick the dandelions on a fine day when the flowers are open. Pick the heads off and measure two quart jugs full.

Wash the flowers very well to remove any insects and put them in a plastic bucket. Slice the lemon and orange thinly and add to the flowerheads.

Pour over them a gallon of boiling water, and stir well. Cover the bucket and leave for ten days, but not longer.

Now strain the liquid off into another bucket and stir in 3 lb. of granulated sugar; stir in the yeast and yeast nutrient. Cover the bucket and leave for another three days.

Strain into a fermentation jar and ferment until dry. You can add a little sugar after a few weeks if it seems necessary.

This wine is very nice when new, but it will improve with age.

ELDERBERRY WINE. FIRST METHOD

> 5 lb. elderberries.
> 3 lb. granulated sugar.
> G.P. wine yeast.
> Yeast nutrient.
> Pectic enzyme.
> 6 cloves.
> $\frac{1}{2}$ oz. well-bruised
>   root ginger.
> 1 gallon cold water.

Gather 5 lb. of elderberries: there are always plenty in the hedgerows. Strip the berries from the stalks; this is easiest to do with a fork; slide it down the stems and push the berries off.

Wash the fruit well, and put it in a preserving pan with a gallon of cold water. Boil until the fruit is tender, then strain off the liquid into a plastic bucket.

Add 3 lb. granulated sugar, 6 cloves, $\frac{1}{2}$ oz. well-bruised root ginger, and stir well. When the liquid is lukewarm, stir in the yeast and yeast nutrient and pectic enzyme.

Cover the bucket and leave for ten days, then strain and ferment. The wine can then be racked and bottled in the usual way.

This wine is very good for colds, especially when taken hot.

It is ready in six months, but better if left longer.

4 lb. elderberries.
3 lb. granulated sugar.
3 cloves.
$\frac{1}{2}$ lb. raisins.
$\frac{1}{2}$ oz. well-bruised
    root ginger.
G.P. wine yeast.
Yeast nutrient.
Pectic enzyme.
1 gallon boiling water.

Pick and wash 4 lb. of elderberries. Strip them from the stalks and place in a plastic bucket. Cut up the raisins and add them to the elderberries, pour over a gallon of boiling water, and stir well. Cover the bucket and leave for two weeks.

Now strain off the liquid into a saucepan and add three cloves and $\frac{1}{2}$ oz. well-bruised root ginger. Just bring it to the boil, and then pour it over the 3 lb. of granulated sugar in a bucket. Stir well.

When the liquid is lukewarm, stir in yeast, yeast nutrient, and pectic enzyme, cover the bucket and leave it for three days.

The wine is then ready to strain and ferment. When fermentation has finished, rack into another jar and allow to clear before bottling.

Ready to drink in six months, but it is much better if kept over a year.

ELDERFLOWER WINE

> 1 gallon elderflowers.
> 3 lb. granulated sugar.
> 1 lemon.
> 1 orange.
> G.P. wine yeast.
> Yeast nutrient.
> 1 gallon boiling water.

After you have cut off the stalks, measure a gallon of elderflowers. Wash the flowers to remove insects, then put them in a plastic bucket with the juice and grated rind of the lemon and orange.

Now pour over a gallon of boiling water and stir well with a plastic spoon. Cover the bucket and leave it for four days. Then strain the liquid off into a saucepan and just bring it to the boil. Put 3 lb. of granulated sugar in a bucket and pour the boiling liquid over; stir well until the sugar has dissolved. When the liquid is lukewarm, stir in the yeast and yeast nutrient.

Cover the bucket well, and leave for another six days, stirring daily. After this time, strain again if necessary and ferment until dry. When fermentation has finished, rack into another jar and allow to clear before bottling. Sweeten with sugar if necessary.

Ready to drink in six months.

44

FIG WINE

2 lb. dried figs.
2½ lb. brown sugar.
½ lb. large raisins.
1 lemon.
1 orange.
½ oz. root ginger.
G.P. wine yeast.
Yeast nutrient.
1 gallon boiling water.

Cut the figs into small pieces and place in a plastic bucket, with the 2½ lb. brown sugar. Chop the raisins and add to the figs. Add the grated rind of the lemon and orange and the juice, but no pith or pips. Bruise the root ginger and add to the other ingredients. Then pour on a gallon of boiling water and stir well with a plastic spoon.

When the mixture is lukewarm, stir in the yeast and yeast nutrient. Cover the bucket and leave for twelve days, but stir daily.

After twelve days it is ready to strain and ferment. Keep in the warm until fermentation has finished, rack and clear before bottling. If the wine is too dry, sweeten to taste with sugar. Stabilize with stabilizing tablets, or sorbital (which can be obtained from any specialist shop) if necessary.

It is ready to drink in six months, but will improve with age.

GINGER WINE

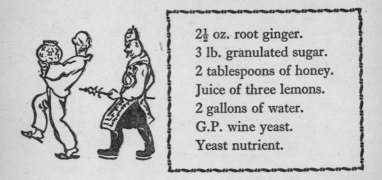

2½ oz. root ginger.
3 lb. granulated sugar.
2 tablespoons of honey.
Juice of three lemons.
2 gallons of water.
G.P. wine yeast.
Yeast nutrient.

Bruise the root ginger well and put it in a saucepan with three pints of water from the two gallons. Bring to the boil and simmer for half an hour. Into a large plastic bucket put 3 lb. of granulated sugar, the juice of three lemons, and two tablespoons of honey. Pour the ginger and water on to this and stir well. Boil the remainder of the two gallons of water and add to the other ingredients, stir it all well, then leave for twenty-four hours. Add yeast and yeast nutrient.

After a further twenty-four hours it is ready to strain and ferment. When fermentation has finished, clear before bottling. You can drink it at once.

I don't waste the root ginger; I put it back into the saucepan with ½ lb. of sugar and a pint of water and boil until the liquid is reduced to syrup. This is useful either to add to hot drinks, or to use as flavouring in puddings or cakes.

3 lb. ripe gooseberries.
3 lb. granulated sugar.
1 gallon boiling water.
G.P. wine yeast.
Yeast nutrient.
Pectic enzyme.

Wash the gooseberries and put them in a plastic bucket. Mash them with a plastic spoon, then pour on a gallon of boiling water. Stir well, then cover the bucket and stand for ten days.

After ten days, strain off the liquid into another bucket, and add the 3 lb. of granulated sugar. Stir until the sugar has dissolved, then add yeast and yeast nutrient and pectic enzyme, cover the bucket and leave it for four days. Stir well every day.

After four days it is ready to strain into a fermentation jar. Fit an airlock and put in a warm place until fermentation has finished. Then rack into another jar and allow to clear before bottling. Never allow the must to sit on the sediment for more than four weeks. If the wine is too dry, sweeten with sugar.

Keep in a cool, dark place for at least six months before drinking, and longer if you can.

GOOSEBERRY WINE.   SECOND METHOD

6 lb. ripe gooseberries.
3 lb. granulated sugar.
½ lb. raisins.
G.P. wine yeast.
Yeast nutrient.
Pectic enzyme.
1 gallon boiling water.

Wash the gooseberries and mash or cut them up into a plastic bucket. Cut the raisins and add to the gooseberries. Add the 3 lb. of granulated sugar and pour over a gallon of boiling water, and stir well.

When the mixture is lukewarm, stir in the yeast, yeast nutrient, and pectic enzyme. Leave for ten days, stirring carefully every day.

After ten days strain off the liquid into a fermentation jar and place in the warm until fermentation has finished. Rack into another jar and allow to clear before bottling. The wine can be sweetened to taste if necessary.

The wine should be ready to drink in six months, but keep it longer if possible!

GRAPE WINE

3½ lb. green grapes.
1 lb. black grapes.
3 lb. granulated sugar.
1 gallon boiling water.
G.P. wine yeast.
Yeast nutrient.

Wash the grapes well and put them into a plastic bucket. Crush the grapes with your hands or a plastic spoon so as not to break the pips. Pour over them a gallon of boiling water and stir well. Cover the bucket and leave it for ten days.

After ten days strain off the liquid into another bucket and add the 3 lb. of sugar, yeast, and yeast nutrient, and stir well. Cover the bucket and leave for another fourteen days, stirring well every day. It is then ready to strain into a fermentation jar.

Fit an airlock and place in the warm until fermentation has finished. Do not leave the must on the sediment for more than four weeks. Rack into another jar, keep in a cool place for the wine to clear before bottling. Leave it for at least six months and much longer if you can, as grape wine improves with age. Inspect it occasionally and add a little sugar if you think it is needed; it shouldn't be, but it largely depends on the ripeness of the grapes.

UNRIPE GRAPE WINE

---

3 lb. unripe grapes.
1 lb. raisins.
2 lb. granulated sugar.
1 lb. demerara sugar.
1 gallon boiling water.
G.P. wine yeast.
Yeast nutrient.

I expect many of you who have grape vines find that in bad summers the grapes will not ripen. There is no need to waste them, as they make a really nice wine. I always use mine this way.

Crush the grapes with the hands, or very carefully with a plastic spoon so as not to break the pips. Put them into a plastic bucket, add the pound of raisins cut in halves. Pour on a gallon of boiling water and stir well.

Cover the bucket and leave it for two weeks. Then strain off the liquid into another bucket and add the 2 lb. of granulated sugar and 1 lb. of demerara sugar, yeast, and yeast nutrient. Stir well until the sugar has dissolved, then cover the bucket and leave for three days, but stir daily.

It is now ready to ferment in the normal way. Taste it after a few weeks and if it seems a little sour, add some sugar to sweeten.

This wine will take nine months at least to mature, but try to leave it longer.

GREENGAGE WINE

3½ lb. over-ripe
  greengages.
3 lb. granulated sugar.
1 gallon of boiling water.
G.P. wine yeast.
Yeast nutrient.
Pectic enzyme.

Wash the greengages and put them in a plastic bucket. It does not matter if some are a bit squashy; they need to be over-ripe to make good wine.

Pour a gallon of boiling water over the greengages and stir them well, then cover the bucket and leave for fourteen days.

After this time, strain off the liquid into another bucket and add the 3 lb. of granulated sugar, yeast, yeast nutrient, and pectic enzyme. Stir well until the sugar has dissolved, then cover the bucket and leave for three days.

It is then ready to ferment in a fermentation jar in the normal way. When fermentation has finished, rack into another jar, put in a cool place to clear. If it is too dry, sweeten with sugar before bottling.

The wine is ready to drink in six months, but like most wines it improves with longer keeping.

HAW WINE

6 lb. haws.
3 lb. granulated sugar.
1 gallon boiling water.
G.P. wine yeast.
Yeast nutrient.
Pectic enzyme.

Pick six pounds of haws; this will not be difficult as there are plenty about in the Autumn. Choose ripe ones.

Wash the haws well and cut off the stalks. Put them in a plastic bucket and pour over a gallon of boiling water, stir well, and try to mash them a little with a plastic spoon. Then cover the bucket and leave for ten days, stirring daily.

Now strain the liquid into another bowl and add the 3 lb. of granulated sugar, yeast, yeast nutrient, and pectic enzyme. Stir until this has dissolved, then cover the bucket and leave for another four days, but stir daily.

The wine is then ready to strain into a fermentation jar, fit an airlock, and place it in the warm to ferment until dry. Rack into another jar to clear before bottling. Keep it in a cool, dark place and taste after a few weeks. Add a little sugar if it tastes a little sour, but it shouldn't need any more.

You can drink it after six months, but keep it longer if possible.

HIP WINE

3½ lb. rose hips.
3 lb. granulated sugar.
1 gallon boiling water.
G.P. wine yeast.
Yeast nutrient.
Pectic enzyme.

This is a really economical wine as the only major ingredient to be bought is the sugar. There are always plenty of hips in the hedgerows; they also contain a large amount of Vitamin C, which I think should be retained in the wine.

Wash the rose hips and cut them in half; put them in a plastic bucket and pour on a gallon of boiling water. Stir them well with a plastic spoon, then cover the bucket and leave them for two weeks.

After two weeks, strain off the liquid into another bucket and add the 3 lb. of granulated sugar. Stir until it has dissolved, then add the yeast, yeast nutrient, and pectic enzyme. Cover the bucket and leave for five days, stirring daily.

The wine is then ready to be strained into a fermentation jar, fitted with an airlock, and put in a warm place to ferment until dry. Rack to clear before bottling.

The wine should be ready to drink in six months, but keep it longer if you can.

LEMON WINE

6 lemons.
1 gallon cold water.
3 lb. granulated sugar.
$\frac{1}{2}$ lb. raisins.
G.P. wine yeast.
Yeast nutrient.
Pectic enzyme.

Wash the lemons, and peel off the yellow rind very thinly so as not to get any pith left on it. Put the rind into a large saucepan or preserving pan with a gallon of cold water, bring it to the boil and simmer for twenty minutes.

Squeeze the juice from the lemons into a plastic bucket containing the 3 lb. of sugar and $\frac{1}{2}$ lb. of raisins. Strain the water off the lemon peel on to the sugar and raisins. Stir well with a plastic spoon until the sugar has dissolved. When cool, stir in the yeast, yeast nutrient and pectic enzyme.

Cover the bucket and leave it to stand for seven days, but stir daily. Then strain it through a piece of muslin into a fermentation jar to ferment. When the fermentation has finished, rack to clear before bottling. After about a month you may need to add some sugar.

It will be ready to drink in about six months, but try and keep it longer.

LOGANBERRY WINE

3½ lb. loganberries.
3 lb. granulated sugar.
1 gallon boiling water.
G.P. wine yeast.
Yeast nutrient.
Pectic enzyme.

Pick the loganberries and wash them well, but do it carefully so as not to lose too much of the juice. Put them in a plastic bucket and pour on a gallon of boiling water, stir well and mash the berries with a plastic spoon. Cover the bucket and leave it for ten days.

After ten days, strain it into another bucket and add the 3 lb. of granulated sugar, yeast, yeast nutrient, and pectic enzyme. Stir until the sugar has dissolved, then cover the bucket and stand for three days, but stir daily.

Now it can be strained into a fermentation jar. Fit an airlock and place in the warm to ferment until dry. Rack to clear before bottling.

It should be ready to drink in about six months, but if you want a really good wine leave it at least a year. You can, if you wish, add a little sugar after three or four weeks.

MANGEL OR MANGOLD WINE

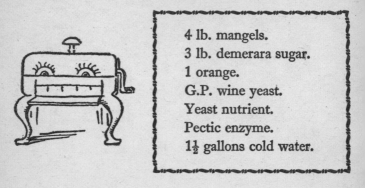

4 lb. mangels.
3 lb. demerara sugar.
1 orange.
G.P. wine yeast.
Yeast nutrient.
Pectic enzyme.
1½ gallons cold water.

You need the humble mangel wurzel or mangold which anyone living in the country should be able to obtain easily enough. Wait until the mangels have had a frost on them as they will make a better wine.

Wash the mangels well, but do not peel them. Slice them thinly into a large saucepan or preserving pan, with 1½ gallons of cold water, or as much water as you can get in. If the pan is not big enough to hold 1½ gallons, add some later as the water evaporates.

Bring to the boil, and simmer until the mangels are tender. Strain the liquid off and throw out the mangels. Put the liquid back into the pan with a sliced orange and 3 lb. of demerara sugar; just bring to the boil, then take off the heat and strain into a plastic bucket.

When the liquid is lukewarm, stir in the yeast, yeast nutrient, and pectic enzyme. Cover the bucket and stand for three days, then strain into a fermentation jar. Allow to ferment and rack to clear in the usual way before bottling. Add a little sugar after six weeks. It is ready to drink in six months but you will find it will be much better later.

MARIGOLD WINE

4 quarts marigold
    flowers.
1 lemon.
1 orange.
3 lb. granulated sugar.
G.P. wine yeast.
Yeast nutrient.
1 gallon boiling water.

Pick the flowers on a sunny day and wash them well to remove any insects. Place them in a plastic bucket. Grate the rinds of the orange and lemon and squeeze out the juice; add this to the marigold flowers.

Pour on a gallon of boiling water and stir well. Cover the bucket and leave to stand for four days. Then strain off the liquid into a saucepan and just bring it to the boil. Put the 3 lb. of granulated sugar into another bucket and pour the liquid over this. Stir well until the sugar has dissolved, then leave it to become lukewarm.

When the liquid is lukewarm, stir in the yeast and yeast nutrient. Cover the bucket and leave for three days, but stir daily. It is now ready to strain into a fermentation jar. Fit an airlock and place in the warm to ferment. Rack to clear as usual.

It will be ready to drink in six months.

MARROW WINE

> 1 ripe marrow.
> 1 lb. demerara sugar to
>   each 2 lb. of marrow.
> Juice of $\frac{1}{2}$ a lemon
>   (approximately – see
>   below) to each 2 lb.
>   of marrow.
> G.P. wine yeast.
> Yeast nutrient.

This is rather an extravagant way of making wine, but as the result is very good, perhaps it can be excused.

Take a really ripe marrow and remove the peel and seeds. Weigh the remainder and cut the flesh into tiny pieces. You may put it through the mincer if you wish. Place in a plastic bucket, and allowing 1 lb. of sugar to each 2 lb. of marrow, cover the marrow with demerara sugar.

Cover the bucket and leave for a week, when you will find the sugar has dissolved and extracted the juice from the marrow. Strain the liquid off into a bucket and add the lemon juice, half a lemon to each pint of liquid. Stir in the yeast and yeast nutrient. Cover the bucket and leave for three days, stirring daily.

It is then ready to strain into a fermentation jar. Fit an airlock and place in the warm to ferment until dry. Try to leave it about nine months at least before drinking as this wine greatly improves with age.

MARROW WHISKY

4 lb. ripe marrow.
3 lb. demerara sugar.
½ lb. raisins.
Juice of one lemon.
G.P. wine yeast.
Yeast nutrient.
1 gallon cold water.

Take 4 lb. of ripe marrow and remove the pith and seeds but do not peel. Cut it into small pieces and put in a saucepan with ½ lb. of raisins and a gallon of cold water. Bring to the boil and simmer until the marrow is tender. Add some more water if it evaporates too much.

Put the 3 lb. of demerara sugar in a plastic bucket and strain the liquid on to it. Add the juice of one lemon. Stir until the sugar has dissolved, and when the liquid is luke-warm, stir in the yeast and yeast nutrient.

Cover the bucket and leave for four days, stirring daily. Strain into a fermentation jar. This wine will need feeding with sugar every two or three weeks. After about six weeks you may find a thick sediment at the bottom of the jar. Strain this off and add some more sugar to the jar. Keep a spare bottle to bring the wine to the top of the jar again.

Ready in six months, but much better if you can keep it longer. It is very good!

MARROW RUM

1 ripe marrow.
5 to 7 lb. of demerara
 sugar, according to
 the size of the mar-
 row.
G.P. wine yeast.
Yeast nutrient.

Choose a really ripe marrow, wipe it clean with a damp cloth, then cut a piece off the stalk end of the marrow, deep enough to enable you to scoop out the seeds and pith from the rest of the marrow. Press the demerara sugar into the cavity left; it depends on the size of the marrow how much you will need; a large one will take about seven pounds of sugar.

Replace the end of the marrow and seal with a piece of sticky tape. Then suspend the marrow over a jar or jug; something with a narrow neck so that the marrow can rest on this but not touch the bottom of the container.

After two or three weeks, unseal the end of the marrow and add some more sugar; some of the first lot will have been absorbed into the flesh of the marrow. Put the end on again and leave for about six or seven weeks, when the sugar should have mixed with the flesh of the marrow and the resulting liquid will have dripped through into the jar leaving only the shell of the marrow. Add yeast and yeast nutrient.

Strain into a fermentation jar, fit an airlock and allow fermentation to finish until dry. Keep the wine at least twelve months, when it will be very strong, much like rum.

MULBERRY WINE

4 lb. mulberries.
3 lb. granulated sugar.
1 gallon water.
G.P. wine yeast.
Yeast nutrient.
Pectic enzyme.

The mulberries are best picked before they are quite ripe. Wash them and put them into a plastic bucket. Crush the berries with a wooden spoon, then pour over them a gallon of boiling water, and stir well.

Cover the bucket and leave it for five days, stir well daily. After five days strain the liquid off the fruit into another bucket. Add the 3 lb. of granulated sugar. Stir well until the sugar has dissolved then add yeast, yeast nutrient and pectic enzyme, and cover the bucket and leave for another three days; stir daily.

The wine is now ready to strain into a fermentation jar. Fit an airlock and place in the warm until fermentation has finished. Then rack into another jar and allow to clear before bottling. Never leave the must on the sediment for more than four weeks as this may affect the taste. If the wine is too dry, sweeten with sugar before bottling.

Keep the wine for at least a year before drinking. The longer you keep it, the better it will be.

ORANGE WINE

4 lb. over-ripe oranges.
3 lb. granulated sugar.
1 gallon of boiling
    water.
G.P. wine yeast.
Yeast nutrient.
Pectic enzyme.

The oranges must be really over-ripe. It doesn't matter if they are mouldy. The wine will be all the better. The greengrocer will usually part with these quite cheaply. He may even give them to you free; mine does.

Slice the oranges into a plastic bucket and pour over them a gallon of boiling water. Stir them well and then cover the bucket and leave for two weeks without stirring. There should be a good mould on top by this time if the oranges were nice and mouldy.

Remove the mould carefully without breaking it if possible, then strain the liquid off into another bucket. Add 3 lb. of granulated sugar and stir until it has dissolved. Add the yeast, yeast nutrient and pectic enzyme. Cover the bucket and leave for four days, but stir daily. The wine is now ready to strain into a fermentation jar. It is then ready to rack and bottle in the usual way.

You may need to add some sugar to each bottle after about a month; taste the wine – if it is still sweet, then leave it alone.

Keep the wine for a year before drinking as it will then be at its best. This really is a lovely wine and very strong. It is a great favourite with many people.

PARSNIP WINE. FIRST METHOD

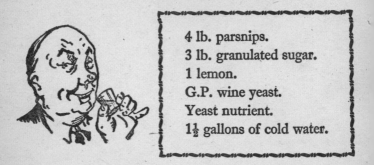

4 lb. parsnips.
3 lb. granulated sugar.
1 lemon.
G.P. wine yeast.
Yeast nutrient.
1½ gallons of cold water.

This wine is best made in February or March with parsnips which have remained in the ground all the Winter.

Scrub the parsnips well, but do not peel them; slice them thinly and put them in a large saucepan or preserving pan. Pour in 1½ gallons of cold water if you haven't a saucepan big enough, cook 2 lb. of parsnips and ¾ of a gallon of water at a time. Cook the parsnips until they are tender, but not mashy. When they are cooked, strain the liquid off.

After straining, throw away the parsnips and return the liquid to the pan. Add the 3 lb. of sugar and the lemon, sliced thinly. Simmer for three-quarters of an hour, stirring occasionally. Strain again into a plastic bucket, and when lukewarm stir in the yeast and yeast nutrient.

Cover the bucket and leave for four days. Then stir it well and strain into a fermentation jar. Ferment until dry, then rack to clear the wine before bottling. If the wine is too dry sweeten to taste with sugar. The wine will be drinkable in six months, but much better if you can leave it longer.

PARSNIP WINE. SECOND METHOD

> 4 lb. parsnips.
> 3 lb. demerara sugar.
> $\frac{1}{2}$ oz. hops.
> G.P. wine yeast.
> Yeast nutrient.
> 1$\frac{1}{2}$ gallons of cold water.

Scrub the parsnips well without peeling them and slice thinly into a large saucepan or preserving pan. Pour on 1$\frac{1}{2}$ gallons of cold water and bring to the boil; simmer until the parsnips are tender but not mashy. Now add $\frac{1}{2}$ oz. of hops and simmer for about half an hour.

Put 3 lb. of demerara sugar into a plastic bucket and strain the liquid on to it. Stir well, and leave until it is lukewarm. Then add the yeast and yeast nutrient. Cover the bucket and leave it for twelve to fourteen days.

Strain into a fermentation jar, fit an airlock and place in the warm to ferment until dry. Rack into another jar and allow to clear before bottling. Add some demerara sugar at intervals of about two weeks until the wine has finished working.

I think the hops give rather an unpleasant bitter taste when the wine is new, but leave it a year or more and then it's a wonderful wine.

PEAR WINE

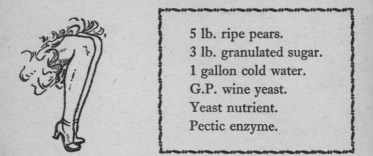

5 lb. ripe pears.
3 lb. granulated sugar.
1 gallon cold water.
G.P. wine yeast.
Yeast nutrient.
Pectic enzyme.

The pears must be very ripe; even the squashy ones will do; this is a good way of using them as pears do go soft so quickly.

Wash the pears or wipe them well with a damp cloth. Do not peel or core them, but cut them in pieces into a large saucepan or preserving pan, and pour on a gallon of cold water. Bring them slowly to the boil, and simmer gently for about half an hour.

Strain the liquid off through muslin into a plastic bucket, and add 3 lb. of granulated sugar and the yeast, yeast nutrient and pectic enzyme. Stir until it has dissolved. Use a plastic spoon for stirring. Cover the bucket and stir daily for three days. Then strain into a fermentation jar.

Fit an airlock and place in the warm until fermentation has ceased. Rack into another jar to clear before bottling. Never leave the wine to sit on the sediment for more than four weeks as this may affect the taste. If the wine is too dry, sweeten with sugar before bottling.

Keep the wine nine months or more before drinking. Store it in a cool dark place if possible.

FRESH PEACH WINE

3 lb. peaches.
3 lb. granulated sugar.
G.P. wine yeast.
Yeast nutrient.
Pectic enzyme.
1 gallon boiling water.

Choose ripe peaches, wipe them with a damp cloth and cut them in halves to remove the stones. Then put the 3 lb. of peaches in a plastic bucket, pour over a gallon of boiling water and stir them well with a plastic spoon. Cover the bucket and stir daily for three days, then leave it covered without stirring for a week.

After a week, strain the liquid off into another bucket and add to it 3 lb. of granulated sugar, yeast, yeast nutrient, and pectic enzyme. It is now ready to strain into a fermentation jar.

Fit an airlock and place in the warm to ferment until dry. When the fermentation has finished, rack into another jar to clear. Always make sure that your equipment is thoroughly sterilized when racking. You can sweeten the wine with sugar before bottling if necessary.

The wine is ready to drink in six months.

DRIED PEACH WINE

2 lb. dried peaches.
3 lb. granulated sugar.
G.P. wine yeast.
Yeast nutrient.
Pectic enzyme.
1 gallon of cold water.

Soak 2 lb. of dried peaches for twelve hours in a gallon of cold water. Then place peaches and water in a large saucepan or preserving pan and bring to the boil; simmer for a few minutes, strain the liquid off into a plastic bucket and add 3 lb. granulated sugar. Stir well until the sugar has dissolved. When the liquid is lukewarm stir in the yeast, yeast nutrient and pectic enzyme. Cover the bucket and stand for four days, stirring daily. Then the wine is ready to strain into a fermentation jar to allow fermentation to continue. Rack and bottle in the usual way.

The wine should be ready to drink in about nine months.

Don't throw away the peaches after you have strained off the liquid; with some sugar added they will make jam. Put the peaches with a little water in a saucepan and add about four pounds of sugar; then stir over a low heat until the sugar has melted; boil quickly until a little jam dropped on to a cold plate wrinkles when the plate is tilted. Then jar.

PLUM WINE

3½ lb. ripe plums.
3 lb. granulated sugar.
G.P. Wine yeast.
Yeast nutrient.
Pectic enzyme.
1 gallon of boiling water.

Choose really ripe plums; any kind will do. Pick off all stalks and leaves and wash the plums, or wipe them with a damp cloth. Put them in a plastic bucket and pour over a gallon of boiling water, stir and mash them with a wooden spoon, then cover the bowl and leave for ten days.

There will probably be a mould on top by this time. Remove this carefully; try not to break any off into the liquid. Strain the liquid off the plums into another bucket and add 3 lb. of granulated sugar, yeast, yeast nutrient and pectic enzyme. Stir well until the sugar has dissolved. Cover the bucket and leave for three days, stirring daily.

The wine is then ready to strain into a fermentation jar to allow fermentation to continue. Rack and bottle in the usual way. The wine should be ready to drink in six months.

You may, if you use really over-ripe plums, leave out the yeast and yeast nutrient, as the wine will be just as good. However it will take longer to mature. In this case, leave it at least nine months, longer if you can.

POTATO WINE. FIRST METHOD

> 4 lb. old potatoes.
> 3 lb. demerara sugar.
> 1 lemon.
> 1 orange.
> Small piece of root
>   ginger.
> G.P. wine yeast.
> Yeast nutrient.
> 1½ gallons cold water.

Wash the potatoes well, but do not peel them. Cut them into small pieces and put into a large saucepan or preserving pan, together with 1½ gallons of cold water. If your pan won't hold this amount, put in as much as you can and add the rest as the water evaporates. Boil the potatoes until they are soft, but not mashy.

Strain off the liquid into a plastic bucket, and add the 3 lb. of demerara sugar, the sliced orange and lemon, and the piece of root ginger. Stir this well until the sugar has dissolved, then return the liquid to the pan and simmer for half an hour.

Now pour the liquid back into the bucket and wait until it is lukewarm. Then add the yeast and yeast nutrient. Stir.

Cover the bucket and leave for three days. Strain into a fermentation jar and place in the warm to ferment in the usual way. Rack to clear and bottle as before.

Ready in six months.

POTATO WINE. SECOND METHOD

> 3 lb. old potatoes.
> 1 lb. raisins.
> 3 lb. demerara sugar.
> ½ oz. hops.
> G.P. wine yeast.
> Yeast nutrient.
> 1 gallon boiling water.

Wash the potatoes but do not peel them. Cut them into small pieces and put them in a plastic bucket. Add 3 lb. demerara sugar, 1 lb. of raisins and ½ oz. of hops, pour over them a gallon of boiling water and stir well with a plastic spoon.

When the contents of the bucket are lukewarm, stir in the yeast and yeast nutrient. Cover the bucket and leave for two weeks, stirring daily. After two weeks, strain the liquid off through muslin into a fermentation jar. Fit an airlock and place in the warm to ferment in the usual way. Be careful not to fill the jar to the top in case the froth should spill out over the top. Wait until the fermentation has subsided before filling to the neck of the jar. Always make sure that the wine is quite stable before bottling. Do this with stabilizing tablets or sorbital, which can be obtained from your specialist shop.

PRUNE WINE

1½ lb. prunes.
3 lb. demerara sugar.
½ lb. raisins.
G.P. wine yeast.
Yeast nutrient.
Pectic enzyme.
1 gallon cold water.

Wash the prunes and put them in a bowl with enough water to cover them and allow for swelling. Soak the prunes for twelve hours, then tip them into a saucepan or preserving pan and add enough water to make it up to a gallon.

Cut the raisins into small pieces and add to the prunes, then bring them to the boil and simmer for about half an hour. Mash the prunes with a wooden spoon while they are cooking. After half an hour strain off the liquid into a plastic bucket and add the 3 lb. of demerara sugar. Stir until the sugar has dissolved.

When the liquid is lukewarm, stir in the yeast, yeast nutrient and pectic enzyme. Cover the bucket and leave it to stand for five days, stirring daily. It is then ready to strain into a fermentation jar. Fit an airlock and place in the warm to ferment in the usual way. The wine is then ready to rack and bottle.

Don't forget to sterilize all equipment before using, as failure to do so could end up with your wine turning to vinegar. Leave this wine for twelve months before drinking.

QUINCE WINE

3 lb. ripe quinces.
3 lb. granulated sugar.
1 gallon of cold water.
G.P. wine yeast.
Yeast nutrient.
Pectic enzyme.

Wash the quinces and cut into four, but do not remove the cores as they will improve the flavour of the wine.

Put the quinces in a plastic bucket, and pour over them a gallon of cold water. Cover the bucket and leave them to stand for seven days.

When the seven days are up, strain off the liquid into another bucket and add the 3 lb. granulated sugar, the yeast, yeast nutrient and pectic enzyme. Stir well with a plastic spoon until the sugar has dissolved; then cover the bucket and leave for another three days but stir daily.

The wine is then ready to ferment in the fermentation jar. Fit an airlock and place in the warm in the usual way. Do not bottle before the wine is clear. Store the bottles in as cool and dark a place as you can find.

The wine should be ready to drink in nine months, but if you want to keep it longer it will be all the better for it.

RAISIN WINE

3 lb. raisins (large ones).
3 lb. granulated sugar.
1 orange.
1 lemon.
1 gallon boiling water.
G.P. wine yeast.
Yeast nutrient.

Cut up 3 lb. of raisins and put in a plastic bucket with the thinly sliced orange and lemon. Pour on a gallon of boiling water and stir well with a plastic spoon. Cover and leave for ten days.

Strain the liquid carefully through muslin into another bowl and stir in 3 lb. of granulated sugar and the yeast and yeast nutrient. Stir until the sugar has dissolved, then cover the bowl and leave for another ten days, stirring daily.

Next strain again and then strain into a fermentation jar. Fit an airlock and place in the warm. Remember not to leave the wine on its sediment for more than four weeks. Repeated racking will help to clear the wine a little quicker. Make sure that the wine is fermented out completely before bottling and you can always sweeten it with sugar if necessary.

The wine should be ready to drink in six months but it will improve if you leave it longer.

RASPBERRY WINE

3½ lb. raspberries.
3 lb. granulated sugar.
1 gallon of boiling
   water.
G.P. wine yeast.
Yeast nutrient.

Pick or buy the raspberries. It does not matter if they are a bit over-ripe, but wash them well to remove any maggots. I find it best to lay them in a bowl of cold water and swish them about gently; if there are any maggots, they float to the top.

Place the raspberries in a plastic bucket and pour over a gallon of boiling water. Stir them well with a plastic spoon. Cover the bucket and leave for ten days.

After ten days, strain the liquid off the raspberries into another bucket and stir in the 3 lb. of granulated sugar. Then add the yeast and yeast nutrient, cover the bucket and leave for another five days. Then strain it into a fermentation jar, fit an airlock and place in the warm to ferment to dryness. The wine is then ready to rack and bottle in the usual way. It is best if you can put this wine in a dark place as the light could fade the colour. If you can't, wrap some brown paper around the jar; this will do just as well.

The wine will be ready in six months.

RED CURRANT WINE

3 lb. red currants.
3 lb. granulated sugar.
1 gallon boiling water.
G.P. wine yeast.
Yeast nutrient.
Pectic enzyme.

Strip the red currants from the stalks, and put them in a plastic bucket. Pour over them a gallon of boiling water and stir well with a plastic spoon. Cover the bucket and leave it for ten days.

Now strain the liquid off through muslin into another bucket, and add the 3 lb. of granulated sugar. Stir well until the sugar has dissolved, then add the yeast, yeast nutrient, and pectic enzyme. Then cover the bucket and leave for another three days, but stir daily.

After the three days it is ready to strain into a fermentation jar. Ferment the wine in the usual way. Again, put the wine in a dark place as the colour is liable to fade. Remember to sterilize all equipment before use and do not leave on the sediment for more than four weeks.

You will find that it will need sweetening before bottling. Redcurrant wine is fairly acid, so you will need to store it for longer than usual.

Redcurrant wine should be ready to drink in nine months, but it will improve immensely if kept longer.

RHUBARB WINE. FIRST METHOD

3 lb. rhubarb.
3 lb. granulated sugar.
1 gallon boiling water.
G.P. wine yeast.
Yeast nutrient.

Rhubarb wine should be made in May or June. Choose big sticks if possible. It doesn't matter if it is a bit tough.

Wipe your sticks with a damp cloth and cut up into small pieces. Place these in a plastic bucket and pour on a gallon of boiling water. Stir it up well, then cover the bucket and leave for ten days.

You will probably find a mould formed by now; remove this carefully without breaking it into the wine. This is easy if the mould is thick. Strain the liquid off into another bucket, add 3 lb. of granulated sugar, yeast, and yeast nutrient, and stir well. Cover the bucket and leave for another three days, stirring daily.

Strain the wine into a fermentation jar and continue as usual. Rhubarb wine can be extremely acid, so you may have to remove some of the acid with precipitated chalk. This is obtainable from your specialist shop or chemist. Use the chalk sparingly as it can remove all the taste of the wine if used to excess. Stir in a dessertspoonful at a time and allow it to settle. The amount used depends a great deal on the ripeness of the rhubarb.

You can start to drink it after six months.

RHUBARB WINE.　SECOND METHOD

> 3 lb. rhubarb.
> 3 lb. granulated sugar.
> 1 gallon of cold water.
> G.P. wine yeast.
> Yeast nutrient.

Some people prefer to make their rhubarb wine by this method. Wipe the sticks with a damp cloth and cut into small pieces; put them into a plastic bucket and bruise them well. Pour on a gallon of cold water and stir for a few minutes with a plastic spoon, then cover the bucket and leave it for ten days.

Next remove any mould, and strain off the liquid through muslin into another bucket. Stir in the 3 lb. of granulated sugar, the yeast and yeast nutrient, then cover the bucket and leave for four days, but this time stir daily. Strain into a fermentation jar. Proceed as in the first method. You will find that by using cold water instead of boiling water the wine will not be so acid.

This will be ready in six months, but will improve if you keep it longer. Rhubarb wine turns out to be a rather dry wine, very clear and sparkling. It is one of my favourites.

RICE WINE

3 lb. rice.
3 lb. granulated sugar.
1 lb. large raisins.
1 lemon.
G.P. wine yeast.
Yeast nutrient.
1 gallon of warm water.

Cut the raisins in half, and place in a plastic bucket with the 3 lb. of rice and 3 lb. of granulated sugar. Squeeze the juice from the lemon and add it to these. Now pour on a gallon of warm water and stir well. Cover the bucket and stand in a warm place for three days, stirring daily.

Mix the yeast and yeast nutrient with a little warm water until it is creamy, then mix with the other ingredients and stir well with a plastic spoon. Then leave for another eight days, stirring daily.

After this eight days, remove the scum from the top and strain the liquid off into a fermentation jar. Place the jar in the warm to ferment to dryness. Rack and clear in the usual way. Rice wine can take a long time to clear, so repeated rackings may be necessary. Remember to sterilize the jars when racking. Rice wine can be very potent, so be careful not to drink too much at a time!

Keep the wine for six months, or longer if you can, before drinking.

SLOE WINE

3½ lb. sloes.
3 lb. granulated sugar.
1 gallon of boiling water.
G.P. wine yeast.
Yeast nutrient.
Pectic enzyme.

The sloes are best picked after a frost, usually about the end of September or the beginning of October.

Gather 3½ lb. of sloes and wash them well. Place them in a plastic bucket and pour on one gallon of boiling water. Stir them round for a while, then cover the bucket and leave it to stand until a thick mould has formed over the sloes. It may take weeks, or even months, but it doesn't matter how long they stand. The thicker the mould the better the wine.

Lift the mould off carefully without breaking it if possible, then strain off the liquid through muslin into another bucket. Stir in the 3 lb. of granulated sugar, the yeast and yeast nutrient, and cover the bucket. Leave for five days, but stir daily. It is then ready to strain into a fermentation jar. The wine is then ready to rack and bottle in the usual way.

It seems to depend on the time this wine is made as to whether it will need sugar added; I have made two lots within a week of each other and found that one needed sugar after a few weeks and the other was still quite sweet. So taste it and add some if you think it needs more sugar. But remember that all wines lose a certain amount of sweetness as they mature. Try to keep the wine a year before drinking.

STRAWBERRY WINE

> 4 lb. ripe strawberries.
> 3 lb. granulated sugar.
> 1 gallon of boiling water.
> 1 lemon.
> G.P. wine yeast.
> Yeast nutrient.
> Pectic enzyme.

Use ripe strawberries. It matters not if they are squashy. Remove the hulls and wash the strawberries to get rid of any earth or dust.

Place them in a plastic bucket with the juice of a lemon and pour a gallon of boiling water over them. With a plastic spoon, mash the strawberries and stir well. Then cover the bucket and leave for a week.

Strain the juice off carefully into another bucket. Don't squeeze any of the pulp through the muslin. Add the 3 lb. of sugar, the yeast, yeast nutrient and pectic enzyme. Stir until the sugar has dissolved, then cover the bucket again and leave for three days, but stir daily.

Now it is ready to strain into a fermentation jar. Then rack and bottle in the usual way. This wine will fade if it is not stored in a dark place. If this is impossible, wrap a piece of brown paper around the jar to keep out the light.

Keep in a cool, dark place for at least six months before drinking.

SUGAR BEET WINE

4 lb. sugar beet.
3 lb. granulated sugar.
1 lemon.
G.P. wine yeast.
Yeast nutrient.
1½ gallons of cold water.

Scrub the sugar beet well, but do not peel. Slice thinly into a large saucepan or preserving pan and add 1½ gallons of cold water. If your saucepan won't hold this amount, put some in and add more as the liquid in the pan evaporates.

Bring to the boil and simmer gently until the beet is tender. Then strain the liquid off through muslin into a plastic bucket and throw away the beet. Return the liquid to the pan and add 3 lb. of sugar and a thinly sliced lemon. Boil for half an hour then strain off into a bucket and leave until lukewarm.

Now stir in the yeast and yeast nutrient, cover the bucket and leave for six days, stirring daily. Then strain and ferment in a fermentation jar. Fill the jar from a spare bottle if the level goes down, as it sometimes will do when wine is fermenting. Rack and bottle in the usual way.

Keep the wine in a cool dark place for at least nine months, when it should be ready to drink.

TEA WINE

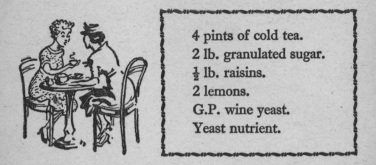

4 pints of cold tea.
2 lb. granulated sugar.
½ lb. raisins.
2 lemons.
G.P. wine yeast.
Yeast nutrient.

Cut up the raisins and slice the lemons thinly. Put them all in a plastic bucket. Add 2 lb. of granulated sugar, then pour four pints of cold tea in. Stir until the sugar has dissolved, then add the yeast, and the yeast nutrient. Cover the bucket and leave it for one month.

After this time you will find a scum on top. Remove this carefully, and strain off the liquid into a fermentation jar to ferment. Rack and bottle in the usual way.

Tea wine can be drunk at once, but I think it is best when kept a few months. Keep it in a cool, dark place.

It sounds strange to make wine from tea, but it does turn out a good wine, tasting not in the least like tea. There is no need to make tea especially for this purpose. If you usually throw away half a pot of tea as I think most people do, just save this up until you have four pints. Strain off the tea leaves though!

I suppose the different kinds of tea and the strength of the brew must make some difference to the wine, so yours will probably turn out differently from your neighbours'.

TOMATO WINE

6 lb. ripe tomatoes.
2 lb. granulated sugar.
½ teaspoon salt.
½ gallon boiling water.
G.P. wine yeast.
Yeast nutrient.

Cut up the tomatoes with a stainless steel knife, or one of those little plastic saw-edged knives which do the job so well. Place the cut tomatoes in a piece of butter muslin and squeeze the juice through into a basin. Pour this over the 2 lb. of granulated sugar in a plastic bucket, add the ½ teaspoon of salt, and pour over half a gallon of boiling water.

Stir well until the sugar has dissolved, allow to cool and then add the yeast and yeast nutrient; cover the bucket and leave for three days. Strain if necessary and then leave to ferment in a fermentation jar. Fit the airlock and place in the warm (about 75°F), and allow to ferment to dryness before bottling. Make sure that the wine is clear when you bottle, thus reducing the amount of sediment in the bottom of the bottle.

Store the bottles in a cool, dark place if possible, anyway in the coolest, darkest cupboard you possess.

Keep tomato wine a year or more before you attempt to drink it.

TURNIP WINE. FIRST METHOD

4 lb. turnips.
3 lb. granulated sugar.
1 lemon.
1 orange.
G.P. wine yeast.
Yeast nutrient.
1½ gallons of cold water.

Scrub the turnips well, but do not peel them. Slice thinly into a large saucepan or preserving pan. Pour in 1½ gallons of cold water, or as much as the pan will hold. You can add some more as the liquid evaporates in the pan.

Bring to the boil and simmer until the turnips are tender but not mashy. Strain off the liquid into a plastic bucket and throw away the turnips. Put the liquid back in the pan, add a thinly sliced orange and lemon, and the 3 lb. of sugar. Simmer for another half an hour. Then strain the liquid through muslin into a plastic bucket. When it is lukewarm, add the yeast and yeast nutrient, and stir it in well.

Cover the bucket and leave for four days, stirring daily. Then strain again if necessary and ferment in a fermentation jar. Make sure that the wine has stopped fermenting before bottling, otherwise the corks might blow out.

The wine is ready in six months, but improves greatly with age.

TURNIP WINE. SECOND METHOD

---

4 lb. turnips.

3 lb. demerara sugar.

½ oz. hops.

G.P. wine yeast.

Yeast nutrient.

1½ gallons of cold water.

Scrub the turnips, but do not peel them. Slice them thinly into a saucepan or preserving pan and pour on 1½ gallons of cold water. Bring to the boil and simmer until the turnips are tender, then add the ½ oz. of hops and simmer for another half an hour. I warn you the place will smell like a brewery while these are cooking!

Strain the liquid off through muslin into a plastic bucket and add the sugar. Stir well until the sugar has dissolved. When the liquid is lukewarm, stir in the yeast and yeast nutrient.

Cover the bucket and leave for twelve to fourteen days, then strain into a fermentation jar, fit an airlock and treat in the usual way.

The turnips taste very strongly and the hops give the wine a bitter flavour at first, but this wears off and the wine is very good if you can leave it nine months or a year. It will probably need some sugar added after a month or so. If you are not sure, it won't hurt to put a small amount in each bottle.

WHEAT WHISKY. FIRST METHOD

2 lb. sultanas.
1 pint wheat.
1 lb. barley.
2 large potatoes (finely grated).
3 lb. demerara sugar.
1 gallon tepid water.
G.P. wine yeast.
Yeast nutrient.

Peel the two large potatoes and grate them finely into a plastic bucket. Add the pint of wheat, 1 lb. of barley, 2 lb. of sultanas and 3 lb. of demerara sugar. Pour on a gallon of tepid water and stir well until the sugar has dissolved. Then add the yeast and yeast nutrient.

Cover the bucket and leave for three weeks, but stir daily. Then strain the liquid off through muslin and strain into a fermentation jar. Fit an airlock and place in the warm to ferment to dryness. Do not leave the wine on its sediment for longer than four weeks. This is a difficult wine to clear, so you may have to rack several times. Sterilize each jar before racking to protect the wine from bacteria in the air.

Bottle when you are sure that fermentation has finished. Leave the wine for at least nine months – much longer if you can – as this is a wine that improves immensely with age. It becomes very much like whisky as it matures.

WHEAT WHISKY. SECOND METHOD

1 pint of wheat.
2 lb. sultanas.
2 large potatoes (finely
   grated).
3 lb. demerara sugar.
Grated rind and juice
   of two lemons.
1 gallon tepid water.
G.P. wine yeast.
Yeast nutrient.

Peel the potatoes and grate very finely into a plastic bucket. Add the pint of wheat, 2 lb. sultanas, 3 lb. demerara sugar, the grated rind and juice of two lemons (no pith), the yeast, and yeast nutrient.

Pour on a gallon of tepid water and mix very thoroughly with a plastic spoon. Cover the bucket and stand for three weeks, stirring daily.

After three weeks, strain off the wine carefully through muslin and ferment in a fermentation jar. Fit an airlock and place in the warm (about 75°F) and allow fermentation to continue until it has finished. Always taste the wine before bottling to make sure that it is not too sweet. If it is, add some more nutrient and place it back in the warm to start fermenting again.

When you are sure that the wine has finished fermenting, bottle. Keep for six months or longer.

WHEAT WINE

> 1½ lb. wheat.
> 3 lb. granulated sugar.
> 1 lemon.
> 1 orange.
> ½ teaspoon ground ginger.
> G.P. wine yeast.
> Yeast nutrient.
> 1½ gallons of cold water.

Put the 1½ lb. of wheat in a large saucepan or preserving pan with 1½ gallons of cold water and bring to the boil. Simmer for half an hour, then strain the liquid into a plastic bucket. Add 3 lb. of granulated sugar, the sliced orange and lemon, and ½ teaspoon of ground ginger. Stir well with a plastic spoon.

When the mixture is lukewarm, stir in the yeast and yeast nutrient. Cover the bucket and leave it for fourteen days, stirring occasionally; then strain into a fermentation jar. Fit an airlock and place in the warm to ferment until dry. Rack into another jar and clear the wine before bottling. Again, this wine may need several rackings before it clears but be patient, it is worth it in the end.

Keep the wine at least six months, and much longer if possible.

PART IV

OTHER DRINKS

BLACKBERRY CORDIAL

> 2 quarts blackberries.
> ¼ pint cold water.
> 1 lb. granulated sugar to each quart of juice.
> 8 cloves.
> ½ nutmeg.
> Wineglass of rum or brandy.

WASH the blackberries and put them in a thick saucepan with a quarter of a pint of water; simmer very gently until the fruit is mashy. Tip the blackberries into a piece of muslin and squeeze all the juice out into a bowl. Measure the juice, and for each quart allow a pound of granulated sugar.

Put the juice and sugar into the saucepan and add the eight cloves and half a nutmeg, not grated. Boil for half an hour stirring all the time. Skim off any scum that forms.

Take the saucepan off the heat and add the wineglass of rum or brandy. Let the cordial cool a little, then pour into warm bottles, put the corks in tightly and, to make sure the cordial will keep, seal the bottles with wax.

This is a very good drink for preventing or curing colds and chills – take a wineglass when necessary.

GINGER BEER

1 oz. root ginger.
1 lb. granulated sugar.
½ oz. cream of tartar.
G.P. wine yeast.
2 lemons.
2 teaspoons caster sugar.
1 gallon boiling water.

Bruise the root ginger and put it in a large bowl with the pound of granulated sugar and the ½ ounce of cream of tartar. Wash the lemons and peel off the yellow rind very thinly, then remove the pith and slice the remainder of the lemons. Add the peel and lemon slices to the ginger, sugar and cream of tartar and pour over a gallon of boiling water.

Stir very well with a wooden spoon, then leave to become lukewarm. Cream the yeast with the two teaspoons of caster sugar and add to the other ingredients. Stir well. I use ordinary baker's yeast for this and find it works as well as compressed yeast.

Cover the bowl and leave for one day, then strain and bottle. Use screw-top bottles or tie the corks on. The ginger beer will be ready to drink in three days. It pops and fizzes just like the shop variety, so I am sure it will be popular with the younger folk.

MEAD

3 lb. honey.
2 whites of eggs.
G.P. wine yeast.
Yeast nutrient.
1 lemon.
1 gallon of cold water.

Put the 3 lb. of honey and grated rind of the lemon in a large saucepan or preserving pan, with one gallon of cold water. Beat the whites of the two eggs until they are frothy and add to the rest of the ingredients.

Place the pan over the heat and stir as the mixture comes to the boil. Then simmer gently for one hour. Pour the liquid into a plastic bucket and leave it to become luke-warm, then stir in the yeast and yeast nutrient.

Cover the bucket and leave in a fairly warm place for three days; stir daily. Then strain through muslin and ferment in a fermentation jar. Ferment and bottle in the usual way.

Store the bottles in a cool, dark place, and keep the mead at least a year before drinking it, as it improves immensely with keeping.

Not many people drink mead now, but it was a very popular drink in olden times.

CIDER

For the best cider, a mixture of different varieties of apples is best. Those usually chosen are non-keepers, small sour or windfalls, with, if desired, a few crab-apples. An odd rotten apple in a large number is permissible, but otherwise they should be sound.

Before the Second World War, my historical searches tell me there were travelling cider presses in some districts, as many farms and cottages had a small orchard. This practice seems to have disappeared, though it may still exist in a few country areas.

To get your apples pressed ideally, a cider factory is the thing, if you can persuade them to do it. Alternatively, a cider factory might sell you the newly pressed apple juice. For those who cannot find a cider factory, you can buy a fruit press from your local specialist shop.

The juice should be put into a wooden cask – a 30-gallon ex-brandy cask is ideal for first-class good keeping cider. Base your calculations on the fact that a ton of apples makes approximately 150 gallons of cider, therefore a cwt. makes approximately $7\frac{1}{2}$ gallons. Any good sized wooden cask is suitable but the larger the better as fermentation goes on longer in a greater quantity of juice, thus producing a higher alcohol content. The cask should stand in a cool place either on its side or end, wherever the bung hole is uppermost.

Never bung up the hole while fermentation is still going on; unless to bring the cask home, perhaps! After about forty-eight hours the apple juice will start to ferment and white froth will bubble up through the bung hole. This will continue for about three weeks. When fermentation has almost stopped, some juice should be siphoned out of the cask with a short length of hose. The amount of juice removed should be sufficient to dissolve the required quantity of sugar.

Add 2 to 4 lb. of sugar (depending on how sweet you want the cider) per gallon *in the cask* to the juice you have removed, and dissolve over heat. When quite dissolved, allow to cool, then return to the cask. Owing to the addition of the sugar there will now be some juice left over. During fermentation, which will go on for about two weeks, the quantity of juice reduces so that you can add gradually (as space permits) the juice which was surplus. When fermentation has nearly finished, if all the 'juice and sugar mixture' is not in the cask, siphon out enough juice to allow this to go in. Then bottle the surplus and use to keep the cask full while the cider is maturing – as the quantity reduces during this process and airspace in the cask will allow bacilli to breed and turn the cider acid. When the juice has completely ceased to 'bubble up' bung the cask up tightly with either cork or wood, and leave for eight months.

Cider is usually made in October–November, and should be left *as long as possible* up to two years before opening it, but at least until the cuckoo sings the following year. Then the cask may be tapped, or the cider bottled down with care.

Innocent to taste but powerful – up to 15% alcohol can be achieved.

BEER

```
3 lb. Malt Extract.
2 oz. hops.
1 lb. granulated sugar.
Top fermenting Beer
    Yeast.
4 gallons of water.
```

This recipe makes four gallons of normal strength beer. If you wish to brew something stronger, cut down the amount of water. If you would like it weaker, then increase the amount of water.

To make half the quantity, halve the ingredients exactly, and, in the same way, if doubling the quantity, see that you double all the ingredients and do not forget any.

To make four gallons, you will need a plastic bucket to hold five gallons. You can make whatever quantity you wish in this bucket, provided that you do not wish to make more than 5 gallons.

Put the hops into a large pot and add 4 pints of cold water. Cover and boil vigorously for 30 minutes. Keep a pinch of hops out to add during the last five minutes of boiling. Meanwhile, put the container of malt extract in hot water to make it run easily and pour the malt into the 5-gallon bucket which you have sterilized.

Sterilization is important. To rinse with boiling water is not good enough. Buy from your chemist or specialist shop 4 oz. of sodium meta-bisulphite and some citric acid. Dissolve the sodium meta-bisulphite and one teaspoon of citric acid in one quart of water and rinse out the bucket with this solution. If you keep the solution in a corked or screw-top bottle, you can use it several times.

Strain the boiling hops over the malt extract, add the sugar and stir until dissolved. Make up the quantity required with cold water, stirring well. When the liquid is cool to the touch, approx. 65°F–70°F, stir in the yeast. Place the bucket in a warm area and cover with a tea-towel.

After two days, a deep froth will appear. This froth will be speckled with dark brown, dead yeast. Remove this froth with a plastic strainer. Do not use metal unless it is stainless steel. The fermentation will continue for 4–6 days. When the fermentation is nearly finished, it is time to siphon into beer bottles.

You can normally tell this when the froth which has covered the top of the beer reduces in size to a ring of about 2 inches diameter, in the centre. A surer way of determining the bottling stage is by use of the hydrometer. Float the hydrometer in the beer, and bottle when it reads 1005. Do not bottle if the reading is over 1010.

A word about bottles. It is advisable to use either beer or cider bottles. The pressure of gas in the beer is sufficient to burst bottles not made for the purpose. You can buy specially designed plastic pressure barrels to dispense your beer. These save a great deal of work washing, sterilizing and filling bottles, and you can pour out a lovely clear pint at will.

If you use bottles, sterilize them with your solution of sodium meta-bisulphite and citric acid, prime the beer by adding $\frac{1}{2}$ level teaspoon of sugar to each pint bottle, and fill to within 1 inch of the top. Stopper the bottles with either crown corks or screw caps and place them in the warm to ferment for two days. After this period, it is better to put the bottles in a cool place. This will speed up the clearing process which should not take more than one week. Finings can be used, but they should not be necessary. The beer can be drunk after two weeks, but it improves if you can keep it another two weeks.

If you are using a pressure barrel, prime the beer by adding $\frac{1}{2}$ oz. of sugar per gallon of beer into the barrel. Place the barrel in a warm place for two days to re-ferment. Loosen the screw cap during this period to allow the gas to escape. After two days, screw the cap down tight and remove the barrel to a cool place to clear. The beer takes longer to clear in the barrel – about two to three weeks, but is all the better for the waiting.

FRUIT SYRUPS. 7 RECIPES

Fruit syrups make a good base for many summer drinks, or with those such as black currant, excellent winter hot drinks for sore throats and colds. These can be made as the various fruits become available and stored in the same way as bottled fruit.

It is best to use the juicy fruits, as it is unnecessary to add water. Any less juicy fruits require a little water added and boiling to extract the juice.

To make certain the fruit syrups will keep, it is best to sterilize them by the water immersion method, as in bottling fruit. Pour the syrup into a preserving jar, screw on the metal top, then give a half turn back to loosen it. Place this in a saucepan of cold water with a folded cloth underneath and bring slowly to the boil. Boil for about twenty minutes, then remove carefully and stand on a wooden surface or dry folded cloth. Screw the top on tightly and leave to cool.

The syrup will retain its colour and flavour better if it is stored in a dark place. It should keep indefinitely. Once the jar is opened, use it up fairly quickly.

BLACKBERRY SYRUP

3 pints blackberry juice.
3 lb. granulated sugar.
2 pints water.

Pick really ripe blackberries. Look them over, remove any stems or hulls and then wash them well.

Place in a saucepan with just enough water to prevent burning – about half a teacup to a pound of fruit. Simmer very gently for twenty minutes. Remove from the heat and mash the berries with a wooden spoon. Strain the juice off through a jelly bag or butter muslin into a jug.

Allow three pounds of granulated sugar and two pints of water to every three pints of blackberry juice. Put the sugar and water in a saucepan and bring slowly to the boil; remove any scum; boil for five minutes; then add the blackberry juice and boil for another five minutes. Remove from the heat and allow to cool before bottling. If you intend to use it in a few days it will keep in bottles, but if it is to be kept for some time then it is better to sterilize it (as was shown above this recipe), otherwise a mould would probably form in the bottle.

Store the syrup in a cool, dark place. This syrup is also a great preventive for colds and chills if taken hot.

BLACKCURRANT SYRUP

> 3 pints blackcurrant juice.
> 3 lb. granulated sugar.
> 2 pints water.

Pick the blackcurrants when ripe. Remove the stalks and wash the currants well. Put them in a bowl and mash with a wooden spoon. Add some boiling water, about half a teacup to 2 lb. of fruit. Mash them again. Then strain the juice off through a jelly bag or muslin.

Measure the juice into a jug. For every three pints of juice allow 3 lb. of granulated sugar, and two pints of water. Put the sugar and water in a saucepan and bring it slowly to the boil, skim off any scum that rises. Boil for five minutes, then add the blackcurrant juice and boil for another ten minutes. Remove from the heat and allow to cool before bottling. Pour it into bottles and seal if you only intend to keep it for a short time. But if you wish to keep it for some time, then it is best to sterilize it in the same way as for bottled fruit. Store it in a dark place.

This syrup is very good for winter coughs and colds; just dilute it to taste in hot or cold water. Also, of course, it contains Vitamin C, which is so necessary to good health, especially for children.

GINGER SYRUP

> 4 oz. root ginger.
> 2 pints water.
> 1 lemon.
> 1 lb. of granulated sugar
>   to every pint of liquid.

Bruise the ginger well – I always break mine into small pieces – and put it with two pints of water in a saucepan. Add two or three thin strips of the yellow rind of the lemon. Boil gently for about three quarters of an hour, then strain through muslin into a jug.

For every pint of liquid allow 1 lb. of granulated sugar. Put all this into a saucepan and add the juice of the lemon. Boil for fifteen minutes, removing the scum as it rises. Leave it to cool, then strain and bottle.

Seal the bottles well, or if you intend to keep the syrup for some time, pour it into preserving jars and sterilize it. This will then keep for years if it is stored in a cool, dark place.

It is a very useful syrup on cold winter days; a little added to a glass of hot water will make a warming drink. It can also be used to flavour cakes and puddings.

LEMON SYRUP

> 1 pint of lemon juice.
> Grated rind of 3 lemons.
> 3 lb. granulated sugar.
> 2 pints of water.

Wash the lemons and grate the rind from them. Squeeze the juice out until you have a pint of juice. If the lemons are warmed first, much more juice can be extracted. Put the grated rind and 3 lb. of granulated sugar in a saucepan with two pints of water. Gradually bring this to the boil, stirring all the time, and boil for ten minutes. Skim if necessary. Pour in the pint of lemon juice and boil for another ten minutes.

Remove the scum and strain the syrup through a jelly bag or muslin and leave to cool. When cool pour it into bottles and seal well, or put in preserving jars and sterilize. Keep the bottles in a cool, dark place.

You may wish to make only half this quantity. If you do, be sure to halve the amounts exactly; it is quite easy to forget some of the ingredients, and, of course, this will put the whole recipe out of balance.

ORANGE SYRUP

> Enough oranges to yield
>   1 pint orange juice.
> Grated rind of 3
>   oranges.
> Grated rind of 1
>   lemon.
> 2 pints of water.
> 3 lb. granulated sugar.

Wash the oranges and lemon; grate the rind from the oranges and the lemon. Squeeze the juice from the oranges until you have a pint. Add the juice of the lemon. Mix the grated rind and the juice together.

Put the 3 lb. of granulated sugar in a thick saucepan with two pints of cold water and bring it slowly to the boil. Boil for five minutes, skimming off any scum that forms. Then add the pint of orange, lemon juice and grated rind, and boil for another fifteen minutes, still removing any scum.

Strain the syrup and, when cool, pour into bottles and seal well. If you intend to keep the syrup for any length of time, it is best to sterilize it in preserving jars.

Keep the bottles in a cool, dark place. They will keep for years if sterilized properly. Once a bottle has been opened, however, it must be used fairly quickly.

RASPBERRY SYRUP

1 pint raspberry juice.
1 lb. granulated sugar.
2 tablespoons water.

Choose nice ripe raspberries and wash them carefully to remove any maggots. Be careful not to lose too much juice while doing this.

Place the raspberries in a saucepan with a thick bottom, with two tablespoons of cold water. Simmer very, very gently until the raspberries are mashy and the juice runs out. Remove them from the heat and mash the berries thoroughly with a wooden spoon. Strain through a jelly bag or muslin and measure the liquid into a jug.

For each pint of raspberry juice allow one pound of granulated sugar. Return the juice to the saucepan with the sugar and bring to the boil. Boil for ten minutes. Remove the scum, strain, and while still hot, pour into hot bottles and seal.

If you intend to keep the syrup for some time it is safer to pour into preserving jars and sterilize in the same way as bottled fruits.

Keep the bottles in a cool, dark place.

STRAWBERRY SYRUP

> 1 pint strawberry juice.
> 1 lb. granulated sugar.

Pick or buy ripe strawberries, but don't use any bruised ones. Remove the hulls and wash the strawberries, then pack them into large preserving jars and stand these in a saucepan of cold water. Place a folded cloth underneath to prevent the jars from cracking, and bring slowly to the boil. Do not screw the jars down. Boil them until the juice begins to run out. This will not take long, as I have found to my dismay when bottling strawberries.

Remove the jars, remembering to stand them on a wooden surface or folded cloth, or the jars will crack. Mash the fruit to extract the remaining juice. Then strain it all through a jelly bag or muslin.

Put the strawberry juice in a saucepan. For each pint of juice add 1 lb. of granulated sugar. Bring slowly to the boil and boil for fifteen minutes, stirring well all the time. Remove the scum, strain into a bowl and leave until cold. Then pour into preserving jars and sterilize. If you intend to use it fairly soon, pour it into bottles and seal the tops.

Keep it in a dark place if possible. It is used for summer drinks with water added.

PART V
CHILDREN'S DRINKS, TEAS AND COFFEE

IT is often a problem to know what to give children to drink in Summer. One can buy endless varieties of beverages but they are mostly expensive. I do not think the cheap ones of the gassy type are very good.

I have collected a few recipes, some of which, if they are a little extravagant, are more wholesome than the manufactured variety. The others are economical and excellent thirst quenchers.

Children appreciate a drink much more if it is made to look attractive. When sometimes I have only one orange or lemon left, with a little ingenuity I have made it up into some sort of drink, and the children have thought it marvellous because it was pretty.

Milk can be made attractive in the same way. My daughters will not drink plain milk at home. They used to force it down somehow at school. I think that is mainly because it looks so dull. Very often I have added a little cochineal and sugar, called it by some exotic name, and it has been swallowed to the last drop, yet the only flavouring was sugar.

I think it especially inviting on a summer day to see a tall glass jug of lemonade, with cool-looking slices of lemon or cucumber floating on top. The floating pieces seem to give it an added charm. I think they have a cooling effect, in the same way as fish swimming in a tank are soothing to watch.

Hot drinks also can be made more appealing by a little deception. My children don't like cocoa made in the usual way – mixed in a cup and hot water poured on – but if I boil it in a saucepan until it is frothy, then call it hot chocolate, they love it. I hope they do not read this, as they will be annoyed to think I have deceived them! It is not the proper thing to do, according to child psychologists. Still, chocolate is made from cocoa, so perhaps I am right after all.

At party times I always mix a fruit cocktail for the children so that they do not feel left out of things while the adults are quaffing wine. It is not much trouble and I like any excuse to concoct a new drink.

I have labelled the following drinks as 'children's drinks', but they need not be confined to children. My husband and I enjoy them, too. In fact, these are one lot of recipes where they were all willing to act as guinea-pigs!

CHOCOLATE MILK WHIP

2 oz. plain or milk
  chocolate.
½ pint fresh milk.
Some cream or ice-
  cream.

This can be made as a hot or cold drink. To make a hot drink put the 2 oz. of chocolate in a pudding basin and stand it in a pan of hot water. Melt it slowly and gradually beat in with a fork the half pint of fresh milk. When the milk is thoroughly beaten in, remove the pan from the heat and using an eggbeater or rotary whisk, beat until the mixture is frothy. Pour it into a glass and add a spoonful of cream; do not stir this in.

To make a cold drink, melt the chocolate in the same way, but only beat in a quarter pint of milk. Take the basin out of the saucepan and beat in the rest of the cold milk. Chill thoroughly, then whisk until frothy. Add a spoonful of ice-cream to the glass. Both these recipes can have sugar added to taste. These make very nourishing drinks for invalids or children who will not drink plain milk. I have only given amounts for one glassful, so the ingredients can be increased in proportion to the number of glasses required.

CHILDREN'S PARTY SPECIAL

1 Tin pineapple juice.
1 Glass of lemon squash.
1 pint of cold water.
1 bottle 'fizzy' lemonade.
A few glacé or maras-
    chino cherries.
Sprigs of mint.
Borage leaves.
1 lemon.

Empty the pineapple juice into a large glass bowl or jug. Add the glass of lemon squash and the pint of cold water and stir well. Pour in a bottle of 'fizzy' lemonade – it can be coloured if preferred and will make the drink look gayer. Slice the lemon very thinly and add it; stir the concoction very gently to mix it well. Add the cherries, maraschino or glacé, whichever you have handy, and some sprigs of mint and borage leaves. If preferred, pineapple pieces can also be added to make it more exciting. Remember to provide spoons as well as drinking straws.

For older children the recipe can be altered a little. Squeeze the juice out of the lemon instead of slicing it, and leave out the mint and borage leaves. Serve the drink in small glasses with a cherry on a stick in each.

ECONOMICAL LEMONADE

---

1 lemon.

½ lb. granulated sugar.

½ oz. cream of tartar.

2 quarts of boiling water.

Sprigs of mint.

This is a good cheap lemonade for those with large, thirsty families. It is very refreshing on a hot, sticky day.

Wash the lemon and slice it thinly, place in a jug with ½ lb. of granulated sugar and ½ oz. cream of tartar. Pour over this the two pints of boiling water and stir well with a wooden spoon. Cover the jug and leave it to cool. Preferably, leave it overnight.

Pour the lemonade into glass jugs and leave the slices of lemon floating on top. Wash a few sprigs of mint and add these to the jugs. Make sure the lemonade is really cold before drinking. If possible, leave in a refrigerator for a while.

This is a good drink for children's parties or picnics. In the summer, my children often asked to have their tea packed to take in the fields, and they liked a large bottle of lemonade each, and often one for their friends. Under these conditions, one bought bottle is no good at all, unless one is feeling rich and can provide a bottle for each! My children usually got the home-made variety.

KIDDIES KOKTAIL

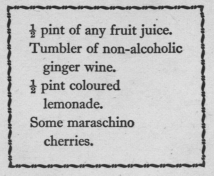

½ pint of any fruit juice.
Tumbler of non-alcoholic
ginger wine.
½ pint coloured
lemonade.
Some maraschino
cherries.

Any fruit juice will do; that strained off stewed fruit, the juice from a tin of fruit, or fresh fruit juice. Fruit syrups mixed with a little water are very good to use.

Put the juice in a jug and pour on the tumbler of non-alcoholic ginger wine, add half a pint of coloured lemonade, matched up to the fruit juice. I find that red is the most popular colour. Mix it all thoroughly. Serve up in small glasses and – to make the children feel quite grown-up – put a cherry on a stick into each glass.

My children insist that the type of glass makes the drink taste different – how true – and they will cheerfully fill a small glass many times rather than save their energy and have one large glass. My youngest daughter even appropriated a small empty champagne bottle, into which she carefully poured her apple wine before transferring it to a glass. She drinks a lot of this when it is new. To me it seems wasted energy, but perhaps my imagination is not so good!

LEMON BARLEY

> 2 oz. pearl barley.
> 1½ pints of cold water.
> 1 lemon.
> 2 tablespoons sugar.

Put the pearl barley in a saucepan with the 1½ pints of cold water and one or two pieces of lemon peel and simmer for about an hour. Pearl barley seems an awkward kind of thing to cook, and the first time I made this drink I found that if I put the lid on, the water boiled over. I left the lid off and forgot it for more than an hour and found the pearl barley had caked in a hard mass on the bottom of the saucepan. So now I compromise. I put the lid half on, and if the liquid seems to be getting dangerously low, I add a little more water. Do remember to simmer very gently.

Strain the barley water into a jug and stir in two tablespoons of sugar and the juice of a lemon. Leave it to cool. Dilute to taste and, if necessary, add some more sugar; it depends whether you have a very sweet tooth.

Do not keep the lemon barley for more than a few days. You may of course use orange juice for flavouring. This is a good beverage for invalids and children, as barley is nourishing and good for the body internally.

MARROW CREAM

> 1 Ripe marrow.
> 1 lb. granulated sugar.
> 1 lemon.
> 1 pint of warm water.
> $\frac{1}{2}$ oz. of yeast.

Cut up about 2 lb. of ripe marrow into very small cubes, omitting the rind and pith. Put the cubes in a bowl and pour over 1 lb. of granulated sugar so that the marrow is completely covered. Cover the bowl and leave it overnight.

In the morning you will find that the sugar has dissolved in the marrow juice; pour this off into a jug. Now pour a pint of warm water over the remaining marrow cubes, stir together for a few minutes, then pour off the mixture into the marrow juice.

Add the juice of the lemon and stir in $\frac{1}{2}$ oz. of yeast. Cover the bowl and leave it in a fairly warm place for about half an hour when you will find it has become frothy. Stir again and it is then ready to drink.

It is best drunk while fresh, as if you keep it for more than a day or two, it will begin to turn into wine. This is quite a health-giving drink, as both the yeast and lemon contain vitamins and the sugar provides energy.

ORANGE AND LEMON COCKTAIL

> 2 oranges.
> 1 lemon.
> 1¼ pints of cold water.
> ¼ pint of hot water.
> Sugar to taste.
> Sprig of mint.
> Sprig of borage.
> Slices of cucumber.

Cut the oranges in half, and squeeze the juice from one and a half oranges. Cut the lemon in half and squeeze the juice from one half. Cut the two remaining halves of orange and lemon into thin slices and put them in a jug with the juice. Add some sugar – two or three tablespoons according to taste. Pour on a quarter pint of hot water and stir well until the sugar has dissolved. Then gradually add the 1¼ pints of cold water.

Float a few sprigs of mint and borage leaves on top, and slide some long strips of cucumber peel down the sides of the jug. Use a glass jug. Chill thoroughly before serving. If your refrigerator is crowded, stand the jug in a bowl of cold water and cover with a damp cloth. Stand the bowl on the floor in a draught.

The mint and borage give the drink an unusual flavour, very summery and refreshing. The children think it is a lovely drink, and it looks attractive with the orange and lemon slices and mint sprigs floating on top.

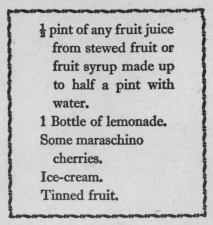

½ pint of any fruit juice
from stewed fruit or
fruit syrup made up
to half a pint with
water.
1 Bottle of lemonade.
Some maraschino
cherries.
Ice-cream.
Tinned fruit.

The fruit juice can be any strained off stewed fruit; see that there are no bits floating. Alternatively, make up some fruit syrup to half a pint by adding water.

Put the half a pint of fruit juice in a quart jug and pour on a bottle of lemonade. Match up the colour and flavour of the fruit juice with one of the proprietary brands of 'fizzy' drinks or use plain bottled lemonade. Mix well. Drop a few maraschino cherries or glacé cherries into the mixture. Add a spoonful of ice-cream to each glass and don't forget a cherry for each one.

To make this more of a party drink, make double the quantity and put it in a large glass bowl. Float pieces of tinned fruit in this, such as pineapple or peaches. Serve up with a ladle and add a spoonful of ice-cream to each glass. Provide each glass with a long spoon and drinking straw.

For a winter party, try leaving out the ice-cream. However, children enjoy ice-cream whatever the weather!

STRAWBERRY MILK SHAKE

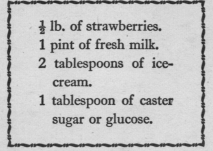

½ lb. of strawberries.
1 pint of fresh milk.
2 tablespoons of ice-cream.
1 tablespoon of caster sugar or glucose.

Wash the strawberries and pick out two of the best looking and put to one side. Lay a piece of muslin in a pudding basin and place the rest of the strawberries in this. Mash them well with a wooden spoon, then lift the corners of the muslin and squeeze the juice and as much of the pulp as possible through into the basin.

Sprinkle on to this a tablespoon of caster sugar – or if you wish it to be more energizing, a heaped tablespoon of glucose; this does not sweeten as much as sugar. Beat this in with a fork and gradually add the fresh milk. Then use a whisk and whisk until it is frothy.

Pour this into two tall glasses. Add a tablespoon of ice-cream and perch a strawberry on top. Provide a long spoon and a straw. If the drink is not very pink, add a few drops of cochineal while whisking.

If you grow strawberries, this is not an expensive drink, and it is one way of getting children to drink milk. I find that when milk is coloured and sweetened, children are more eager to drink it.

ORANGE REFRESHER

> 1 orange.
> 1 Tumbler of orange squash.
> 1½ pints of cold water.
> Sprigs of mint.
> Cucumber peel.
> 1 tablespoon of sugar.

Put the tumbler of orange squash in a large jug with the one and a half pints of water. Squeeze the juice from half the orange and add to this. Cut the other half into thin slices and float on top.

Stir in a tablespoon of sugar and drop in a few sprigs of mint. Cut a few strips of peel from a cucumber and slide down the side of the jug. Cool thoroughly before drinking. The cucumber and mint give it an added flavour.

You can of course use lemon squash and a lemon if you prefer, or grapefruit. Another way is to mix them; use half of each squash and either half each of the orange or lemon, or use both and add some more water.

A few lumps of ice dropped in make it a much more refreshing drink on a hot day. A good cooling mixture to use in the absence of a refrigerator is a handful of washing soda and a handful of cooking salt in a little water. Stand the jug in this for a while.

HERB TEAS

Many folk grow herbs in their gardens, especially the commoner ones such as mint, sage, thyme and marjoram. These, if made into tea, all have some special medicinal property, known for hundreds of years by the gypsies and country folk.

I have tried some and they certainly do work. They are not all very pleasant to taste, but I find if one sips them while very hot, the flavour is not so pronounced.

Some leaves and flowers of other plants are also used in this way; most are made by pouring hot water on the fresh or dried leaves and leaving the brew to stand for a few minutes in the same way as ordinary tea.

So after reading the following recipes and their healing properties, you can go and search in the garden for the cure for your special ailment, and save on chemist's bills. Of one thing you can be sure, if they do not bring relief they can do no harm. I am the guinea pig in this family; if I survive and have no ill effects from drinking a new concoction, then the others will consent to try my wonderful mixtures – that is, if they do not taste too horrible!

The children quite like taking the coltsfoot cough mixture, as the honey and lemon disguise the taste of the coltsfoot leaves. Do not try to keep this for too long; I bottled some once and forgot it for a while; when I next looked, it had turned into wine, but I didn't like it very much. So you see, almost anything will make wine. I have heard of people using vegetable peelings. But I am wandering from the subject.

There are a great many other herbs found growing wild, which at one time were used as medicines, and many are still used as the basis of modern medicines. But as these would need a book on their own, we will keep to the ones which most of us know.

Some of the herbs, such as sage and thyme are evergreen, but I always dry some. With things like mint which just disappear in winter, it is important to dry enough for winter use, unless you can grow it in a greenhouse or in pots indoors. It is so much easier to take them from a jar in winter than trample around a muddy or snow-covered garden to pick what you need.

The most usual way of drying herbs is to hang them in bunches in a warm room and leave them to dry. I think they get dusty this way, so I wash mine and dab the leaves dry with a cloth, then spread them out on tins and dry slowly in an oven, electric setting 200 degrees. It takes hours, and one must be careful not to over-dry them. Leave the oven door open slightly to let the moisture escape quickly. When they are dry the leaves can easily be stripped from the stalks and stored in screw top jars.

I keep one jar of mixed herbs for cooking, ready for stuffing or any other savoury; it saves getting out a whole array of jars and taking a little from each. The home grown herbs smell so much better than the shop ones.

BLACKCURRANT TEA

This is very good for colds, and as a preventative or relief for sore throats.

If the blackcurrants are in season, boil those and use the juice with some sugar added. But colds are not so prevalent when blackcurrants are ripe; I expect if you have blackcurrants in the garden you make jam from them, or if not buy a good brand from the shop. A tablespoon of this jam in a glass of hot water is a quick way to make a soothing drink. To make it more nourishing for an invalid, add the jam to a glass of hot milk.

COLTSFOOT TEA

This is very good for coughs; I can recommend this as we have often taken it.

Gather a few leaves of coltsfoot; they are big and thick, rather like an overgrown primrose leaf; so you will not need many. Put them in a saucepan with a pint of water and simmer for twenty minutes. Add the juice of a lemon and some strips of peel, and simmer for another five minutes. Strain the liquid off and sweeten to taste with honey or brown sugar. It can be kept for a few days, but as I have said before, it will turn into wine if it is kept too long.

CARAWAY SEED TEA

These can be grown in the garden. The plants look very much like carrots while growing. The seeds are good for flatulency, and from the taste of caraway seed tea, I should imagine that gripe water for babies is made from the same thing. With a little sugar added, the tea is quite a pleasant drink. I like it, but then I always did pinch the baby's gripe water!

Crush the seeds, or buy the already rolled ones; you will need half an ounce to half a pint of water. Put the seeds in a jug and pour on half a pint of boiling water, stir well, then cover the jug and leave to stand overnight. I usually add some sugar when the mixture is hot. Strain the liquid off and bottle it. Put the cork in tight. Do not keep it for more than a week or so. It is best to make a small amount and have it fresh. A spoonful of this will relieve the 'wind'.

CARROT TEA

This is supposed to relieve gout. I don't suffer from it – not yet, anyway, so cannot vouch for the cure, but I have been told that it is good.

Scrub a large carrot and slice it thinly into a saucepan, and add half a pint of water. Put the lid on and boil for forty minutes. Strain off the carrot liquid and drink a cup of this night and morning.

I expect the treatment would have to be continued for some time to have any effect.

CAMOMILE FLOWERS TEA

These are for clearing the blood and to relieve headaches. The dried flowers can be bought from the chemist.

Put a pinch of the flowers in a cup and pour on boiling water. Cover the cup and leave it for about five minutes, then drink it while still hot.

CELERY TEA

This is good for rheumatism, they say, either the stalk or the seed can be used.

Boil a few stalks of celery or $\frac{1}{2}$ oz. of seed in a pint of water for about half an hour, then strain the liquid off and take a glass every day.

I believe eating raw celery is meant to be equally beneficial, but some people find this hard to digest.

CLOVE TEA

This is also good for flatulency.

Put four or five cloves in a small cup and pour on boiling water. Crush the cloves a little, then cover the cup and leave for five minutes. Sip it while it is hot.

HOP TEA

Hops seem to be a cure for numerous complaints. They act as a tonic, a cure for indigestion; to regain a lost appetite and many other things. No wonder beer is so popular! Taken hot, hop tea is a cure for sleeplessness.

Put a handful of hops in a jug and pour on a pint of boiling water. Cover the jug and leave until cold. Take a small glassful when necessary.

MARJORAM TEA

This is said to relieve headaches.

Put a teaspoon of marjoram leaves, fresh or dried in a teacup and pour on boiling water. Cover the cup with a saucer and leave for about five minutes, then sip it while hot.

MINT TEA

This is also good for headaches and helps to relieve flatulence. I think it is quite pleasant to drink.

Put a few leaves, dried or fresh, into a cup and pour on boiling water. Cover the cup and leave for a few minutes. Sip it while hot. For flatulence, add a pinch of bicarbonate of soda.

RASPBERRY LEAF TEA

This is also good as a gargle for sore throats and many people believe that it helps in making confinements easier if taken regularly beforehand. I do not know if doctors agree with this, but it is a very widely known remedy.

Pick a handful of raspberry leaves, or use dried ones. Put them in a jug and pour on half a pint of boiling water. Stir well, then cover the jug and leave for five minutes. Some people prefer to put the water and leaves into a saucepan and bring to the boil, as they say that more of the goodness of the leaves is obtained this way. Always drink the tea hot, but cool it a little of course for a gargle.

ROSEMARY TEA

Here is yet another cure for headaches. It also makes a good hairwash.

Pick a few rosemary flowers and put them in a cup. Pour on boiling water, and cover the cup with a saucer and leave to infuse for five minutes. Sip slowly while hot. For a hairwash, make larger quantities and use as a rinse.

SAGE TEA

This can be used as a gargle or as a hairwash; it is supposed to darken the hair and prevent greyness.

To make it, you need a handful of fresh or dried sage leaves, placed in a jug and a pint of boiling water poured over. Stir well, then cover the jug and leave it to get cold. Strain, and use as a gargle or hairwash.

STRAWBERRY LEAF TEA

This is said to relieve diarrhoea.

Pick and wash a handful of strawberry leaves, and put them in a cup. Pour on boiling water and press well with a spoon, then cover the cup and leave for five minutes. Sip it while hot.

THYME TEA

This is a very good relief for whooping cough. A little taken when the cough is troublesome is said to bring speedy relief. It can also be used as a gargle for sore throats.

Put a small teaspoonful of fresh or dried thyme leaves in a cup and pour on boiling water. Cover the cup and leave it for a few minutes to infuse, then sip it while hot, or cool it for a gargle.

DANDELION COFFEE

This is not a herb tea, but as it is a drink, I thought I would include it. I have been told that dandelion roots make very good coffee, very much like the real thing. It is quite simple to make. Scrub the root, then bake it in a slow oven until it is quite dry. Grate it very finely, then use in the same way as coffee. I always mean to try it, but when I think of it I never seem to have a fork handy to dig the root. If the price of coffee goes up any more, I certainly shall give it a try.

INDEX

Amounts, 17
Apple wine, 25
Apricot Wine (fresh), 27
Apricot Wine (dried), 28

Basic amounts and methods, 17
Barley wine, 29
Beet wine, 83
Beetroot wine, 30
Beer, 96
Blackberry Cordial, 91
Blackberry syrup, 100
Blackberry wine, 31
Blackcurrant syrup, 101
Blackcurrant tea, 120
Blackcurrant wine, 32
Bramble wine, 31
Bullace plum wine, 33

Calendar for winemaking, 22–24
Camomile flowers tea, 122
Caraway seed tea, 121
Carnation wine, 36
Carrot tea, 122
Carrot wine, 34
Celery tea, 122
Cherry wine, 35
Children's Party Special, 110
Children's Drinks, 107
Chocolate Milk Whip, 109
Christmas Drinks, 20
Cider, 94
Clearing the wine, 14
Clove Carnation wine, 36
Clove tea, 123
Coffees, 107, 125
Coltsfoot tea, 121
Coltsfoot wine, 37
Cowslip wine, 38
Currant wine (black), 32
Currant wine (red), 76

Damson wine:
    First method, 39
    Second method, 40

Dandelion wine, 41
Dandelion coffee, 125
Dried apricot wine, 28
Dried peach wine, 68

Economy, 10
Economical lemonade, 111
Elderberry wine:
    First method, 42
    Second method, 43
Elderflower wine, 44

Fermentation, 13
Fermentation jar, 14
Fig wine, 45
Forming a mould, 12
Fresh apricot wine, 27
Fresh peach wine, 67
Fruit syrups, 99–106

General hints on winemaking, 9
Ginger beer, 92
Ginger syrup, 102
Ginger wine, 46
Gooseberry wine:
    First method, 47
    Second method, 48
Grape wine, 49
Grape wine (unripe), 50
Greengage wine, 51
Guess what, 20

Haw wine, 52
Herb teas, 119
Hints on winemaking, 9, 21
Hip wine, 53
Hop tea, 123

Kiddies' Koktail, 112

Lemon barley, 113
Lemon syrup, 103
Lemon wine, 54
Lemonade, 111

Loganberry wine, 55
Lucky Dip, 20

Mangel wine, 56
Mangold wine, 56
Marigold wine, 57
Marjoram tea, 123
Marrow cream, 114
Marrow rum, 60
Marrow whisky, 59
Marrow wine, 58
Mead, 93
Metal containers, 10, 11
Methods, 17
Mint tea, 123
Mould, forming a, 12
Mulberry wine, 62

Orange and lemon cocktail, 115
Orange cocktail, 21
Orange refresher, 118
Orange syrup, 104
Orange wine, 63

Parsnip wine:
    First method, 64
    Second method, 65
Peach wine (dried), 68
Peach wine (fresh), 67
Pear wine, 66
Plum wine, 69
Plum wine (bullace), 33
Poppets' Punch, 116
Potato wine:
    First method, 70
    Second method, 71
Prune wine, 72

Quince wine, 73

Racking, 16
Raisin wine, 74

Raspberry leaf tea, 124
Raspberry syrup, 105
Raspberry wine, 75
Red currant wine, 76
Remedies – Wines as, 19
Rhubarb wine:
    First method, 77
    Second method, 78
Rice wine, 79
Rosemary tea, 124

Sage tea, 124
Sloe wine, 80
Sterilization, 12
Storing wine, 16
Straining the wine, 14
Strawberry leaf tea, 125
Strawberry milk shake, 117
Strawberry syrup, 106
Strawberry wine, 81
Sugar beet wine, 83

Tea wine, 84
Teas, 107, 119–125
Thyme tea, 125
Tomato wine, 85
Turnip wine:
    First method, 86
    Second method, 87

Unripe grape wine, 50
Utensils and containers, 12

Wheat whisky:
    First method, 88
    Second method, 89
Wheat wine, 90
Wine making – general hints, 9
Winefly, 13
Wines as Remedies, 19

Yeasts, 17

Basic Freezer Recipes

Uniform with this book

SAVE—SAVE—SAVE

Freezer ownership transforms the housewife's cooking habits. Find out how to save money, time and work by 'chain cooking'. All the answers are in this book. How to prepare meals before freezing. How to use the cheaper cuts of meat. How to cook multiple meals in one go. How to store them. The freezer housewife can cook her dinner party food weeks before the date so as to spend a relaxed and unrushed evening with her guests.

150 super mouth-watering freezer recipes. Included: freezer space needed: maximum storage times: soup: fish: poultry: meat: puddings: cakes: all covered. A must for every housewife and mum.

Right Way to Make Jams

SAVE—SAVE—SAVE

With the ever-increasing cost of commercially manufactured jams and conserves, more and more folk are making their own.

No need for a garden of your own – make huge savings by buying fruit and vegetables in bulk – follow these recipes and make yourself and your family superb jams, conserves, marmalades, curds, pickles, chutneys, and ketchups. All included in this money-saving book.

Uniform with this book

This is only a small selection from the wide range of *paperfronts*. A full catalogue can be had by sending S.A.E. to the address below.

ELLIOT RIGHT WAY BOOKS
KINGSWOOD, SURREY, U.K.